THE POWER COUPLE

Navigating The Roller Coaster Of Business With Your Soulmate While Raising A Family

**DR. RICHELLE PEÑA and
DR. WILLIAM A. PEÑA**

To our children, Adrian, Leia, and Annabelle, we hope that you can obtain wisdom from the experiences we endured. Always remember to put God first in your lives and pursue your own dreams with passionate dedication.

Table of Contents

PREFACE

William Peña

LIFE IS AN INTERESTING paradox. I could not fathom that as a four-year-old boy who immigrated to this country and experienced poverty during my early years, I would one day run a multimillion-dollar business with my wife, all while raising three beautiful kids and traveling the world with them. To me, this all still seems surreal, and I am grateful for the opportunities that God has offered me.

Our incredible entrepreneurial story began more than a decade ago when my wife, Richelle, and I decided to build a business centered around children's dental care. We saw the inherent need for dental offices that catered to the underserved populations—patients with Medicaid insurance or those with special needs—and we decided to focus our business on providing access to care to all children regardless of dental insurance or medical condition.

Although our hearts were in the right place, we went through our share of mishaps, hardships, and setbacks, not only in building our company, but in our personal lives as well. Fortunately, we found solace and strength in one another, and were able to succeed in running our business—and ultimately selling it—while also raising a close-knit, loving family.

Both Richelle and I believe that the success we share in many facets of our lives happened because of our strong conviction that we could actually accomplish it. Ever since I can remember, Richelle and I have always manifested our belief that we could be successful running our business, nurturing our marriage, and raising our children. Since we wholeheartedly believed it was possible, we focused all our attention and efforts in actually accomplishing these goals. As we consistently remind our children, and as you, the reader, delve into this book and reflect on your own personal journey, it is crucial to remember that your *attitude* ultimately determines your *altitude*.

Though, it is also important to note that our story is merely an illustration of what *worked for us* as soulmates going into business together. We recognized the loving and collaborative nature of our personal relationship and felt that we could harness our strengths to establish and operate a business as a team.

When I mention collaboration, I am emphasizing that Richelle and I have consistently made equal contributions to every aspect of our shared journey, including our marriage. There is no such thing as being dominant or submissive in our relationship; we see each other as being part of a *team*. Furthermore, we view our relationship as being synergistic in nature, where the relationship is stronger than either of us individually—hence why we refer to ourselves as a "power couple."

Once we made the decision to join forces to build our business together, we understood that having a clear plan in place would not only help us avoid conflicts and disagreements but also provide us with a sense of direction and purpose.

With this in mind, we developed a framework for our partnership that encompassed the following key elements:

1. **Clearly Defined Roles and Responsibilities**: We outlined specific roles and responsibilities for both our personal and professional lives. This ensured that each of us had a clear understanding of our individual responsibilities and areas of expertise, minimizing the potential for confusion or overlap.

2. **Mutual Respect and Boundaries**: We made a commitment to respect each other's authority and not overstep boundaries. This meant acknowledging and valuing each other's opinions, decisions, and areas of expertise, and refraining from micromanaging or undermining each other's authority.

3. **Pursuit of a Common Vision**: We agreed to work toward a shared vision for our business. This involved aligning our goals, values, and aspirations, and constantly communicating to ensure that our actions were in line with our shared vision.

4. **Open and Honest Communication**: When confronted with an issue, either at home or at our company, we would discuss it and offer candid suggestions of what happened, who was responsible, and how we can ameliorate the situation to prevent it from happening in the future.

By implementing this blueprint, we were able to establish a harmonious partnership that allowed us to navigate both the challenges and successes of our business and personal lives. It provided us with the clarity and confidence needed to drive better results and create a thriving business, while also nurturing our marriage and family life.

Richelle and I also came to the realization that in any team-based environment, it is crucial to have a clearly designated leader who possesses the ability to make final decisions. We recognize the significance of this because the presence of ambiguity and the absence of clearly defined leadership roles can result in unnecessary conflicts and, ultimately, breed resentment. We were determined to prevent this drama from infiltrating our marriage and business partnership. As a result, we made the deliberate choice to assign leadership roles based on suitability and compatibility.

For example, at our company we both agreed that it would make sense for me to lead the organization since I am a pediatric dentist and we were opening a *dental* business. Richelle, in turn, would lead the training and marketing efforts of the company since she had corporate experience from working at Target Corporation.

Conversely, at home, Richelle is the "C.H.O." or chief home officer, and she is responsible for our social activities, travel itinerary, and managing our home (liaising with contractors for repairs, paying the bills, etc.). My role at home is to help provide financially for our family and enforce our mutually agreed upon rules.

We strongly advise individuals who are contemplating starting a business with their life partner to conduct a thorough evaluation of their existing relationship and assess whether they are really compatible as business partners. It is crucial to consider factors such as communication styles, decision-making processes, and the ability to separate personal and professional matters. By conducting this honest assessment, individuals can make an informed decision about whether embarking on a business venture together is the right choice for them. Ask yourselves, *Do you currently work well together taking care of issues that arise at home? If you have kids, do both parents contribute equally in raising the children? How well do you know your partner? Do you or your spouse get easily flustered when something does not go the way you expected? What is the personality type of you and your partner? Dominant? Submissive? Supportive? Analytical? Do you know what makes your partner sad, angry, or happy?*

We understand that making this decision can be daunting, and you may be uncertain about whether working together is the right choice for you. Our hope is that by reading our book and learning about our journey, you will gain valuable insights to help you determine if working with your spouse or life partner is a feasible option for you. By sharing our story and discussing what worked (and what didn't work) for us, we hope to provide you with guidance and inspiration as you navigate this important decision.

If you come to the realization that you and your life partner have a strong working dynamic and have always desired to start a business together, we firmly believe that you have the potential to achieve remarkable success. By capitalizing on each other's strengths and fostering synergy, you can create a powerful partnership that propels your business forward.

Personally, running our business with my wife has been one of my greatest professional accomplishments by far. She is not only an amazing leader who demonstrates empathy and compassion to others, but she is also ambitious, confident, and driven. She was also my support during difficult times when the pressures of the business began affecting my health. Without her, I am not sure if I would've had the wherewithal or the motivation to continue.

As a disclaimer, much of what we present in our book is from our own recollections and from facts gathered from our family and colleagues from work. We will try our best to present information as we remember it. Some names and characteristics have also been changed, some incidents have been partially fictionalized to protect the anonymity of the individual, some events have been compressed, and some dialogue has been recreated.

In addition, our unwavering faith in God has been a cornerstone of our journey. We firmly believe that our success in both our business and personal lives is a direct result of our reliance on our faith. We approach our work as a calling from God, and we strive to honor

Him in all that we do. While our faith is rooted in Christianity, we understand that individuals may have different beliefs or spiritual practices. Regardless of your own beliefs, we encourage you to find a source of inspiration and guidance that resonates with you and aligns with your values. This could be a higher power, a spiritual practice, or simply a personal philosophy that brings you peace and purpose. By incorporating this element into your relationship and business, you can find strength, resilience, and a deeper sense of meaning in your journey.

INTRODUCTION

Richelle Peña

B ACK IN 2011, Will asked me to join him on his dental startup business. Although I was excited at the prospect of working together and the value our collaboration could bring to our business, I was also apprehensive that our partnership could negatively affect our marriage and our family. After conducting a thorough evaluation of our personal relationship and engaging in deep introspection, akin to the approach suggested by Will in the preceding section, we concluded that we possessed the necessary qualities to form an effective partnership. We firmly believed that by joining forces, we had the potential to create an extraordinary company.

Although working with my husband proved to be challenging at certain points throughout our journey, especially when we were growing and managing a complex business and jointly raising a family, it was well worth the effort. For starters, we relied heavily on each other especially during those turbulent times as new parents and business owners. We supported each other when having to work long hours, when we needed to have critical conversations with our team members, when making important and life-altering decisions, and when facing dilemmas (trust me, there were quite a bit of these). We also motivated and supported one another during those difficult nights when our kids were sick and crying, and throughout the stressful moments in our business when we thought that we would lose everything.

Now that I have given you a brief synopsis of our entrepreneurial journey, let us go in a little deeper and talk about *you*. Are you a business leader? Do you have a significant other that is a leader in his or her career? Are you thinking of starting your own business with your life partner? If the answer is yes, then this book is for you, but it will take a lot of commitment to become your version of a power couple. It also takes a lot of hard work, sacrifice, perseverance, and most importantly, passion, to survive in the world of business.

Take inspiration as you read through our story, though, and remember that you don't have to endure the difficult path of entrepreneurship by yourself. If you and your significant other determine that you could actually work together without creating any strain in your personal bond or with your loved ones, you have the potential to unlock incredible synergies in every aspect of your lives.

I consider myself fortunate to have had my husband, Will, as my business partner. Together, we experienced both challenges and successes on our journey, which I will share with you shortly. However, through it all, we emerged as successful entrepreneurs, better equipped to balance our roles as parents to our children, and we forged a deeper personal connection between us.

When we faced difficult moments during our tenure as entrepreneurs, I often sought out books that would help me juggle all my responsibilities at home and at work. Most books I encountered solely focused on business; others on raising a family. I have yet to find one that combined both. We were inspired to write this book to showcase our amazing journey—our roller-coaster ride—of starting and managing a business together and including our experiences of also being parents and a married couple.

Do you think you are capable of working alongside your spouse or life partner while having responsibilities at home with your kids? If you are unsure at this point, don't be discouraged! The reason Will and I wrote our book is to offer you the opportunity to explore this possibility.

In my opinion, who said you cannot do it all? Who said you have to choose either being a parent or being an entrepreneur? Who said it is impossible to work with your significant other? If you live life doing what people think you should do, then you won't ever be able to live to your fullest potential. Learn to overcome your fear and start making an impact with your life. If you picked up this book, then I know you are looking for a resource to teach you to become a better leader, not just in business, but in all facets of life. Books have been the key to our learning and evolution as business leaders and in our personal self-improvement throughout the years.

Our story is written as a stream of consciousness based on our experiences as a married couple, entrepreneurs, and parents. Our goal is to show you that it's not only possible to build a successful business with your significant other, but it's also possible to pursue other priorities, such as being an involved parent, achieving a fitness goal, etc. at the same time.

We also strongly believe that you are more than capable of achieving balance in your personal and work life, and you can live your life to its fullest potential without having to pick one thing that you are passionate about while sacrificing others. Life is not a zero-sum game. You can be an entrepreneur *and* a parent *and* a loving life partner *and* a good friend *and* pursue your own personal interests, such as fitness, fashion, etc.

Admittedly, some of the topics and suggestions proposed in our book to become a better parent and successful leader inevitably require you to step outside your comfort zone, but this discomfort is often the biggest key to growth. In fact, we believe that the real magic happens in the *uncomfortable* zone.

If you are afraid, unsure, or even overwhelmed by the thought of working with your life partner, we encourage you to silence your mental chatter and first read this book. If you ultimately decide that you and your spouse are capable of working together but don't know where to begin, we recommend simply taking the first step. As Laozi states in the *Tao Te Ching*, "A journey of a thousand miles begins with a single step." Take that first step in faith and the universe will conspire to help you navigate your own roller coaster of marriage, business, and parenthood with your soulmate.

Chapter One

Humble Beginnings

Richelle Peña

I REALIZED AS AN adult that the person I am today is because of how my family raised me as a child. The decisions that I've made, my personality traits, and my positive outlook on life are all attributed to the teachings and experiences that I've lived through with my parents, siblings, grandparents, aunties, and uncles. My family has played an important role in shaping the strong, independent woman I am today, so it's only natural that I start this book with my origin story.

I come from humble beginnings, and like Will mentioned in the preface, I could never have imagined I would be where I am today. Both of my parents hail from the Philippines and like most Filipinos, they are both nurses. My parents both came to the United States during the time when the country contracted nurses from abroad. If you ask anyone who is Filipino, they are probably a nurse, or someone in their family is a nurse. Was it my parents' dreams to become nurses? Probably not, but because of the necessity to leave their homeland for a better future, they chose this career as a way out.

My father, Ricardo, is a highly respected individual within the Filipino community. He possesses excellent communication skills, is pragmatic, and exhibits a wealth of knowledge. Interestingly, he had initially enrolled in seminary school in the Philippines with the intention of becoming a priest. However, due to the extreme poverty he experienced back home, he made the difficult decision to leave the seminary after four years of study and pursue a career in nursing. It was during his time at nursing school that my dad crossed paths with my mother, Tessie.

Unlike my dad, who is more quiet and reserved, my mother possesses a vibrant personality. She is talkative, persistent, and displays an exceptional level of empathy toward others. Her selflessness and nurturing nature make her the epitome of care and compassion. As I reflect upon my own character, I realize that I am a perfect blend of both my parents' remarkable traits.

My mother is from a small rural village approximately two hours away from Manila. Recognizing the limited possibilities of breaking free from poverty, she made the decision to pursue a path of studying nursing and relocating abroad as her sole means of escaping her current circumstances. Given the lack of educational options available in her village, she opted to attend a high school in a town located an hour away, which would provide her with the opportunity to eventually enroll in a nursing school in the capital city.

My mom eventually met my dad while living in Manila and they both decided to leave behind the harsh living conditions of their native land to move to the United States in search of a better life, not just for themselves but also for their families back home.

*My parents, Ricardo and Teresita Garcia, were college
sweethearts and moved to the United States in 1977.*

My parents quickly learned how to make a good living in the
United States and worked two shifts at the hospital. In due course,
my father would ascend to the position of nursing manager. After my
parents worked as nurses in the hospital for almost ten years, they
took the leap of faith and opened their own nursing agency. Their
nursing agency staffed some of the major hospitals in Miami-Dade
County. The hospitals would hire my parents' nursing agency to meet
their staffing needs, and this was the turning point for them. They
built a successful business that gave them the financial freedom to live
in one of the best neighborhoods, send us to top-rated schools, and
provide us with a path to success.

Although my parents both worked full-time, I never felt like I was
missing out on my time with them because they always knew how to
balance work and family time together. Every Sunday was sacred, our

family day. We would go to church and then out to lunch. We would also have dinners every night as a family and talk about our days.

My parents have had a huge influence on my life. I learned to prioritize my family over work, and I also saw the importance of having dinner together every night to talk, learn something, laugh, and share incredible moments from our days. I especially loved our dinners because my family had the opportunity to be together after a hectic day. With my own family nowadays, I have continued this tradition. We have dinner as a family, during which we go around the table and each share our experiences from the day and what we are grateful for.

My grandparents also played a major role in my life growing up. When my parents found out they were having me, they petitioned my grandparents, who were living in the Philippines at the time, to move to the United States to help take care of me and my two siblings. My grandma, Nanay, was like my second mom. She was always around to take care of me and was very loving. My grandpa, Tatay, was the cook in the house. He made delicious Filipino dishes like chicken adobo and pancit noodles with rice. They lived with us until I was in first grade and were a big help to my parents. It takes a village to raise a family!

I admire my parents for having the courage to leave their family behind to come to a foreign country in search of a better economic opportunity. Their tales of perseverance through countless hardships, coupled with their eventual triumph in their nursing-agency business, served as a profound source of inspiration during my formative years. These stories instilled in me a deep sense of responsibility to honor their sacrifices by diligently pursuing my education and ensuring that their efforts in paving the way for our family were not in vain.

As I grew older, despite being surrounded by many family members who were nurses, I realized that nursing was not the career path I wanted to pursue. Instead, I made the decision to study fashion design at Florida State University (Go Noles!) because it was a field that I was truly passionate about. I also wanted to immerse myself in the college experience by attending a large campus and joining a sorority.

During my freshman year, as part of my fashion design curriculum, I took a biology course and surprisingly excelled in it, earning one of the highest grades in the class. This achievement made me reflect on my aspirations of being a fashion designer. *Was I really going to be the next Vera Wang?* It also made me question whether I should consider a career in healthcare, a path commonly chosen by Asian-Americans. I also started feeling homesick halfway through the semester, which prompted me to reevaluate my life choices.

After careful consideration and taking my parents' recommendation into account, I made the decision to move back home and pursue a career in pharmacy. While I recognized that pharmacy offered financial stability and a lucrative salary right after graduate school, deep down, I knew that it was not my true passion. Instead, it was a practical choice to ensure a stable future.

Little did I know back then that my pharmacy career would give me the tools I needed to succeed in our own business.

William Peña

I was born in the northern Caribbean coast of Colombia in the beautiful, portside city of Barranquilla on July 2, 1980. My father, Antonio, moved to Miami when I was only twenty days old to establish a better life for us in America. After my dad established himself, he petitioned my mom, Ana, and she moved three years later to join him. I moved to the United States in 1984 when I was four years old.

My parents and I eventually settled in a suburb of Miami known as Hialeah. My parents were poor but were fixated on becoming successful in order to provide for our relatives back home and give me and my siblings a better life in the United States. I saw my parents as individuals who were not defined by their circumstances, their perceived lack, nor their language. My dad happened to come to Miami during the time that a mass exodus of Cuban and Colombian nationals landed in south Florida. This period in south Florida's history was marked not just by high unemployment, but also rampant crime. The cocaine wars of the early '80s marked a period of instability and lawlessness in Miami. Living here was like living in the Wild West. Hearing shootouts between rival cartel members and seeing dead bodies in a dumpster or in homes under construction was not unusual.

Furthermore, being Colombian during the '80s and '90s in Miami carried with it a negative stigma, and my family and I were often referred to as "drug dealers." Despite the sly and sarcastic remarks made by others based on my parents' nationality, I saw that these comments never had any real impact on them. On the contrary, I saw how proud my parents were of being Colombian, and this influenced me to follow suit. Living my entire life with the negative stereotype of being a "Colombian drug dealer," I was not only accustomed to it, but I vowed that instead of being ashamed of my background I was going to represent it with pride. To this day, although I grew up in America and have been in this country for almost forty years, I can speak Spanish with native fluency and identify myself with other Colombians back in my homeland.

My parents had a hard time finding work when they arrived in Miami during the '80s. Since there was a large influx of immigrants during that time, there was a scarcity of jobs. Rather than lament or become sour over the grim situation, they persisted and eventually found work as night custodians at a now defunct gymnasium known as Sportsrooms. Since we were alone in this country, and for fear of leaving me alone in our apartment, my parents would take me to the gymnasium and lay me to sleep on two adjoining chairs. At dawn, we would drive home, and I would get ready for school. After dropping me off at my school, my parents would drive to their second jobs— my dad was a dishwasher at a restaurant, and my mom worked as a seamstress at a factory.

By the time I was an adolescent, my parents were able to save enough money, and with the financial help of my paternal grandfather, who had recently arrived from Colombia, they were able to acquire a kitchen cabinet business. They worked extremely hard in that factory, working virtually nonstop, hardly ever taking a break.

Antonio Peña and Ana Jimenez, my beloved parents. They immigrated from Colombia in search of a better life and encountered the "Cocaine Cowboys" era of South Florida during the 1980's

My dad is an old-school, Latino alpha-male who wanted me—his first-born son—to be as tough and hard-working as he was. He would always remind me that I would have a family one day and that it was a man's job to take care of his wife and kids; therefore, he said he needed to raise me to be strong. Growing up with my father was like attending the School of Hard Knocks on how to become a man. Although my dad was hard on me and his child-rearing ways were a bit unconventional, I learned a lot of life lessons from him.

When I was eleven, I really wanted to attend a summer camp with my friends from school. It was a camp where we would play games, have fun, and eat popsicles. It was the usual kid-friendly, fun summer camp that most children attend after school ended. I could not wait until school ended so that I could attend camp with my buddies. I asked my dad a few weeks before classes ended, and he flat out denied my request. He mentioned instead that I was old enough to start working at his cabinet factory. I was flabbergasted, but I had no choice. Beginning in the summer of 1991, and every summer throughout middle and high school (and weekends, too), I would work at my parents' factory.

When I first started, I was tasked with removing the wood dust from the different machines at the factory. As I got older, I was assigned the role of "cabinet cleaner," which entailed removing the industrial-grade adhesive that permeated the cabinetry. This seemingly innocuous process actually involved using an acetone-based solvent known as mineral spirits that would cause second-degree chemical burns on my young hands. The burn was so bad that I would literally stick my hands in the freezer to soothe the pain. When I told my dad and showed him my hands, he simply motioned for me to wear gloves and to stop complaining.

When I was around fifteen years old, I was "promoted" to cabinet installer. My job was to assist my uncle, Fabio, with kitchen cabinet and bathroom vanity installations. It was a laborious task, and I especially hated this particular job since it oftentimes involved long days at construction sites in homes with no air-conditioning. If you have ever been to Miami in the summer, you know how hot and humid it gets here!

I remember on one dreadful occasion, a rusted nail pierced the underside of my foot, causing blood to trickle down my shoe. I was rushed to the urgent care for fear that I may contract tetanus and received a booster shot. On a separate occasion, I almost cleaved the middle finger of my right (dominant) hand with a table saw. On all these occasions, I was simply told to "man up"; basically, I could not demonstrate any sort of weakness. In our culture, whining and complaining is frowned upon and not typical male-like characteristics.

Admittedly, these experiences seem to be atypical for any teenager to endure and may even be considered borderline abusive, but they were among my greatest life lessons. At the time, I hated that I had to go to work every weekend and summer at my dad's factory. I would dig in my heels and complain—to no avail—to my parents. My dad has an intolerance for excuses, and when I asked, "But why do I have to go to work when all my friends get to have fun during their time off from school?" he would simply respond, "Because I am teaching you to be responsible and to know the meaning of hard work. I don't want you growing up spoiled and entitled. Besides, you have responsibilities here at work, so stop asking me to let you hang out with your friends. The answer is *no*!"

The experience of working at my parents' factory also taught me several things. The first lesson I learned was that I was going to work my ass off in school so that I could attend college and become a professional. I knew for certain that I never wanted to work in construction or in a factory. The second lesson was that having been exposed to such harsh conditions during my entire adolescence, I understood the meaning of hard work and perseverance. This served me well, especially in dental school, when I had to put in hours in the library studying for exams. If I could endure chemical burns, rusty nails, and having my finger nearly sawed off, I could definitely endure my grueling study sessions! Lastly, and perhaps the most important, was that witnessing how hard my parents worked to make their nascent business a success taught me the value of determination and hard work in pursuing my own dreams.

Because my parents had worked so hard and established valuable relationships with home developers and contractors early on in their careers, they were fortunate to ride the construction boom that Miami experienced during the late '80s and throughout the '90s, causing their business to flourish during that period. I was proud of what they had achieved—despite all their perceived limitations—and I vowed to follow their example in my own life.

After high school, I attended the University of Miami (Go Canes!) on a scholarship, and I also continued working for my dad (now as a kitchen salesman) to pay for my personal expenses. I studied hard, took the admissions test to get into dental school, and earned a high enough grade to grant me the opportunity to attend the dental school of my choosing. Because I am so family oriented, I decided to stay home and attend the dental school at Nova Southeastern University, a mere fifteen-minute drive from my parents' home, which was where the next important phase of my life began.

Chapter Two

Soulmates

William Peña

URING MY SECOND YEAR of dental school, I met the woman I knew I was going to marry from that first moment. Richelle and I first met at a Halloween party being hosted by the health professions division of our university. At the time, she was a first-year pharmacy student, and she looked absolutely stunning in her Hawaiian hula dancer costume, replete with a coconut bra and grass skirt. I was stunned by how gorgeous she looked in her costume. When our eyes locked across the room, we both felt an immediate, powerful connection. I know it sounds sappy and cliché, but when you have an immediate connection with someone and you feel like kindred spirits from the very first moment you meet, you know that you are destined to be together. After all, you share an unbreakable bond.

She walked past me, brushing my arm as she did, and then turned around and gave me a little wink and a smile. I am naturally shy and introverted, but knowing that she was smitten by me, I immediately became poised and confident.

I quickly approached her, and for reasons I still do not understand, I introduced myself as "William"—not Will or Willy, like I am usually referred to, but "William." She asked me almost incredulously, "Your name is . . . William?" and I nodded approvingly. "William? That's your name?" Then she continued in her characteristic plucky manner, "Based on how you look, I thought your name would be 'Raul.'" I could not help but laugh at this seemingly prejudicial comment. Admittedly, although I was in dental school, I maintained my goatee and fade, and looked more like a baseball player than a dental student.

After a brief prefatory conversation about our respective health-care programs at the university, I casually asked her if she had a boyfriend. She snapped, "Sorry, but you came too late into my life. I already have a boyfriend!"

Undeterred, I replied, "Look, that doesn't matter because in the end I know you'll end up with me."

To this day, I cannot fathom how cavalier I was when I first met Richelle. I have a self-effacing, polite demeanor, and am usually not so forward with people. Shortly after that fateful event, Richelle ended her relationship, and we began dating. We have remained inseparable till this day.

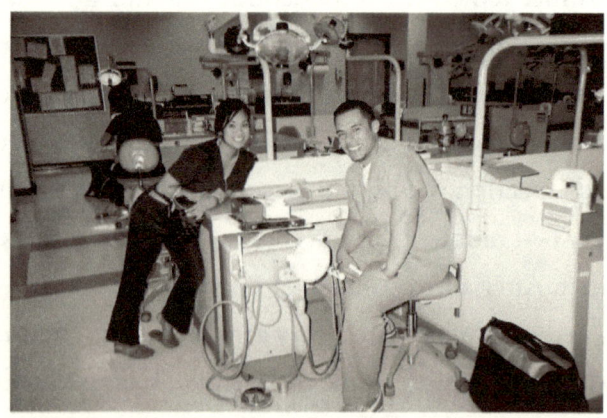

Richelle and I met in graduate school at the Health Professions Division (HPD) at Nova Southeastern University. Richelle would oftentimes stop by the dental simulation lab to visit me.

I eventually graduated dental school and moved to California to attend the pediatric dentistry program at the University of California, San Francisco (UCSF). Prior to moving to California, I proposed to Richelle. We were married two years after we got engaged on December 15, 2007. Our wedding was one of the most memorable moments of my life. I was marrying my best friend and someone who truly understands who I am at the core.

After that, I graduated with honors from UCSF in July of 2009. Eleven years after graduating high school, I had earned a bachelor's degree, two master's degrees, a doctorate degree, and I had just finished my advanced training program in pediatric dentistry. I had also successfully passed the first part of the board exam to become board certified in pediatric dentistry. I was proud of myself and grateful that God allowed me to accomplish so much up to that point.

I had worked hard, learned a great deal, applied myself, and now I was ready to begin my professional working career as a pediatric dentist. Along with my mind overflowing with business ideas and Richelle by my side, I was ready to take on the world!

Chapter Three

California Livin'

Richelle Peña

WHEN I GRADUATED FROM the pharmacy program at Nova Southeastern University in 2007, I moved to San Francisco to be with Will while he finished his residency at UCSF. Although I had graduated from pharmacy school, I still needed to take the license exam in California in order to practice as a pharmacist. While I took and passed the law exam, I took a job as a pharmacy intern at a Target pharmacy. As a pharmacy intern, you could basically do everything a pharmacist does except the final check and sign-off on a prescription to be dispensed. I worked hard to show them I was a team player, excellent with patient care, and was willing to do anything to help the pharmacy team.

Little did I know that my hard work was being noticed by my superiors. As soon as I passed my pharmacy law exam, I was offered a promotion as an executive team leader—or pharmacy manager—in Pinole, California.

I freaked out. *Why me? Are they sure?* I had never had a "real" job prior to this, let alone led anyone in my life. I didn't know what a pharmacy manager's responsibility entailed, but I knew I could learn anything. I was twenty-five years old with no business experience, and I would now be running my own pharmacy. Despite my fears, I told myself, *You got this!* and accepted the position.

Although I was nervous about being in charge, I quickly became comfortable in my newfound position, namely because I had so much passion and fire to learn. I managed two pharmacists—one who was about to retire, and another younger pharmacist that was a little older than me. Although I was the youngest person in the pharmacy—and was now the pharmacist in charge—I remained confident in my abilities to lead my team. I decided that I would be kind and supportive toward my team members. I had a prior boss who many pharmacists before me had labeled as an "asshole," and I witnessed firsthand why he had earned such a deprecating title. He was impatient, apathetic, and chastised me and the staff on numerous occasions when we asked him for help. I cried many times because of his leadership approach, and I vowed to never treat my direct reports in such a condescending manner. When I became the boss of my pharmacy, I decided to lead with love. It was easy to do, admittedly, because they were such great people. They were self-sufficient, pleasant to talk with, and very responsible. I learned that having the right people on my team made my life simple.

My Pinole pharmacy quickly became one of the best pharmacies in the district. We had high patient satisfaction scores, high script count (which meant higher revenues), and our team morale was outstanding.

Because of my performance, I was being pulled away from my routine pharmacy duties by my managers so that I could be a resource to pharmacists in underperforming stores. My manager would assign me to these stores in order to turn around their operations and get these stores to become more successful. I was even part of several pharmacy acquisitions.

I also got the opportunity to attend Target Business College (TBC). During my time at TBC, I got certified to conduct proper interviews using situational-based methods. The purpose of this certification was to allow me and other certified managers to interview and hire prospective pharmacists and interns. It was a wonderful tool to use since rather than asking simple "yes/no" or leading questions, I would find out more about the person—and how they would act or react in certain scenarios—by asking situational-type questions. I found this approach to be so valuable, that I decided to use it for our hiring practices in the dental business that I co-founded later on with Will. I will provide more details about our business and partnership with Will at a later time.

While working at Target, I started loving the business side of pharmacy and felt that this aspect of my job allowed me to shine and have a more meaningful impact.

I also loved living with Will in a brand-new city. We lived in San Francisco together for two years (Will had moved to California a year prior to me joining him since he graduated from dental school a year earlier than me). We explored different food spots around the city, took the monthly pilgrimage to Napa Valley to go wine tasting, and simply enjoyed the vast culture that is prevalent throughout this wonderful coastal city. It was a time where we really got to know one another. We learned what made us "tick," and we learned our likes and dislikes.

As an example, I learned that Will loves sleeping in arctic-like conditions, and he would often leave the windows to our small apartment wide open, letting the frigid air come through. I also discovered my art of cooking, and I would often play chef in the kitchen, preparing culinary delicacies such as homemade apple pie and seafood risotto, and traditional Colombian and Filipino dishes such as *arepas, carne guisada con papas, pancit bihon, kare-kare,* etc.

After Will completed his post-graduate studies at UCSF, we took a celebratory trip to Greece and Egypt. It was a personal gift to both of us to celebrate the graduation from his residency program and the start of our professional careers. I believe you have to celebrate the "wins" in your life. You have to grind hard, but you also have to stop, reflect, and commemorate your accomplishments. It cannot be all work and no play. Our motto is, work hard but play *harder*. You have to maintain a balance.

We spent almost three weeks in Greece and Egypt in the summer of 2009. It was hot, especially in the Sahara Desert of Egypt, but we were so enamored with all the historical landmarks, the architecture, and the food that we paid little mind to the sweltering heat beaming down on us. We were awestruck by the ancient relics that have been around for thousands of years.

This trip to such exotic destinations also awoke our wanderlust spirit. We spoke extensively about how we wanted to eventually travel with our children and take them to see the world.

But first, it was time to settle down and start our life together back in Florida, where Will would start his new job as a dentist.

Chapter Four

The Real Word

William Peña

RICHELLE AND I FINALLY moved back to Florida in the summer of 2009. We were still on a high from our recent trip to Greece and Egypt, and we were excited to be around our family and friends again. I was also excited to start my new job as a pediatric dentist in an established practice. I had big dreams and wanted to accomplish so much. I was eagerly counting down the days to start. This new job was an opportunity to change the world, as I saw it, and make a positive impact. I was ready to begin changing lives and believed that I was working in an office that shared in my benevolent vision. I was in for a rude awakening.

During my years in pediatric dental residency at UCSF, I witnessed firsthand the difficulty that many parents had in accessing a pediatric dentist for their children. Many of them had to travel for hours to university clinics or non-profit centers because there were no dentists in their communities that accepted Medicaid. I was crestfallen at this reality and saw it as a personal calling to help families that needed access to a dentist and had little to no recourse. I wanted to use my skills as a pediatric dentist to serve communities that were either shunned or neglected.

When I moved back home to Florida, I purposefully sought out a dentist that accepted Medicaid, since I felt that there was a great need in this area and I figured that any dentist willing to accept this type of insurance at their office had their heart in the right place. Perhaps it was naiveté or simply that this man was completely irreverent, but the experience of working for this dentist was the worst "best" experience of my life because it taught me what *not* to do while treating patients and running an office.

First of all, I was appalled at the humiliating and disgraceful manner in which this individual treated his team members. He treated them as lesser beings that were hired solely to serve him and his every need, in whichever way he pleased. It was terrible to witness this spectacle, and I felt even worse for his staff, who were honest, hard-working individuals.

Worse yet, he treated his young patients in the most inhumane manner possible. He treated them in such a horrid manner that I used to come home heartbroken. On one occasion, he told a five-year-old boy who was getting a cavity filled, and was understandably scared lying in the dental chair, that if he did not stop crying, he was going to put the needle of the anesthetic syringe up his nose. I was taken aback and appalled by the dentist's jarring comment and the disgraceful manner in which he treated an innocent child who was simply frightened.

The child began crying hysterically, and this man did not give two hoots about how this young child felt. He had no empathy and no compassion whatsoever. He simply went about his way laughing and flirting with his young dental assistant.

I had a one-year contract with this individual, and I literally counted down the days until my contract expired. I was miserable and hated going to work. I had a severe case of the "Sunday Blues," and I became sad and anxious on Sunday evenings in anticipation of having to go into work on Monday mornings. Although I earned good money, I could not suppress my own morals and ethics to work for an individual who was so snobbish and heartless.

I decided that I would not endure this misery any longer nor put my good name and reputation on the line being associated with an individual and office like this, but I needed a fallback plan. My original plan was to work at least two years as an associate and then open my own business. But given the tenuous situation with my employer, I sure as heck was not going to renew my employment agreement for another year. I needed to pivot and come up with plan B, and pronto.

Given the tense situation, I decided to begin the process of opening my own dental practice early. I spoke to Richelle, explained our options—purchase an existing practice or open a brand new office from the ground-up—and we both agreed on the latter.

From the onset, I was not interested in acquiring a dental practice from a retiring dentist. When you acquire an existing dental office, you will have patients on the schedule (which is a huge plus) and cash flow from day one, but there is the possibility of inheriting a dilapidated office, ripe with old, malfunctioning equipment and, potentially, toxic team members.

There was also a scarcity of pediatric dental practices coming up for sale in the marketplace, and I didn't want to wait around until one became available. Another point, I wanted to pick my own location to build an office rather than letting a sales opportunity dictate where I should practice. So, I decided instead to open a brand-new office in a suburb I knew well, since I had attended high school while living there.

The only problem was I had no clue where to obtain financing, how to construct a dental office, where to find the real estate, etc. There were so many unknowns! I had no idea where to start. Rather than get discouraged by the magnitude of the project, I did what I always do when confronted with a difficult situation. I decided to break up the problem into smaller, more manageable tasks and attacked each in sequential order.

I asked an acquaintance, a pediatric dentist, which bank he had used for financing. He forwarded me his banker's contact information, and I called him the next day. I introduced myself and gave him a synopsis of what I wanted to do (build an office from the ground up, and own—not lease—the real estate). We set up a lunch meeting the following week, and I proceeded to send him my personal financials. He never asked me for a business plan, but I figured that a large loan like the one I was requesting would require a plan of how I intended to use the funds. I procured a beautiful business plan chock-full of facts, figures, charts, bar graphs—the works! I even went ahead and bound the copy of the business plan so that it would look more professional. I even came up with the name of the office—American Pediatric Dental Group—a name that represented my lofty ambitions of establishing dental clinics across the country.

Richelle accompanied me to the lunch meeting, and after some small talk with the banker, he proceeded to casually tell me that I was already approved for the business and real estate loans; our mouths dropped almost in tandem! Furthermore, he told us it would require no money down from us, and in fact, the loan also included working capital. We were stunned, to say the least.

After he dropped this bombshell of news, I sheepishly pulled out the business plan and handed it to him. He quickly glanced at it, flipped through a couple of pages, handed it back to me, and simply told me, "Nice." Nice?!? After all the time it took me to create this wonderful masterpiece, he barely even looked at it. But hey, he was financing our first dental office, so I was definitely not going to complain!

I was proud of myself for taking the entrepreneurial leap *and* finding a bank that believed in me and was willing to finance my dental practice. From there, we pushed onward.

Chapter Five

Facing New Changes

William Peña

BASED ON MY CONVERSATIONS with the banker, architect, and the general contractor that I interviewed, the project would take at least a year before it was completed. I decided to find a different job in the meantime prior to my new office opening. Under no circumstance was I going to continue working with my current employer. Before handing in my resignation letter, however, I decided to search for new job opportunities. I knew that I could not work at another dental practice because the hiring process for a new dentist at an office is usually between two and four months, and I had way less time than that on my existing agreement with my employer.

One day at work, I decided to call my former mentor and chairman of pediatric dentistry at Nova Southeastern University and ask him if there were any employment opportunities available at the school. He told me that he was, in fact, looking for a clinical professor, and we set a meeting at his office for a couple of days later. I arrived at his office and discovered the dean of the school, along with a couple of other faculty members, in attendance. I am not going to lie, it was a pretty intimidating scene. They had apparently read over my resume and were impressed. They wanted to know if, instead of a full-time clinical professor position, I would be interested in becoming the program director of the residency program since the current director was retiring.

I was honored, to say the least. I was being offered a prestigious position by a chairman and dean whom I had known for a long time and truly admired and respected. But, I told them that I would need time to think it over, and they agreed to give me a couple of days. I spoke it over with Richelle, but we agreed that opening our business, rather than pursuing a career path in academia, would be best suited for us. I called the chairman and politely declined his offer, but mentioned that I was still interested in the clinical professor position. Without hesitation, he offered me the job.

The only problem was that my salary would take a significant hit. Luckily, Richelle intervened and told me, "Will, I know how miserable you are at your current job. I make good money working at Target, and our personal overhead is low. Go ahead and take the job at Nova, and don't focus so much on how much you will be making. I know it's a significant reduction in salary, but sometimes in life you have to take a step backward to take two, strong steps forward. You know that you will eventually have your own office, and you will earn a lot more than simply being an associate at someone else's practice. Don't lose sight of the big picture."

She was right. After consulting with Richelle, I made the decision to resign from my job and take on an academic position in the interim.

To this day, I am so happy I made the decision. That job experience proved to be an invaluable experience for me, one that would help me immensely as a leader at our own company.

For starters, it taught me to have patience with individuals that are just starting off and perhaps lack confidence. By being patient, properly explaining the assignment to my students, allowing them to ask me questions and make mistakes, and then providing constructive feedback, I created a safe environment where real learning took place. I knew that this was a great way to share ideas and communicate new information with others, and this helped form the framework of my "no-asshole" policy at work.

Both Richelle and I had horrible and ineffective bosses prior to opening our business, and we both vowed to be different types of leaders—servant leaders—where we would always be a resource to our team and not chastise them for asking us questions or reaching out to us for help and guidance.

As for our personal lives around this time, at the end of 2010, after living a year with Richelle's parents, we decided to move to a condo in Sunny Isles Beach, a picturesque beach city in Miami-Dade County.

On the day we were moving into our new waterfront condo, we stopped by our local Publix grocery store to purchase cleaning supplies. Richelle casually informed me, "Babe, I'm late."

I responded, "Late for what? We don't have to be in the condo for another hour. We are actually early for a change."

She quickly replied, "No, silly, I haven't gotten my monthly visitor!"

It finally dawned on me what Richelle was referring to, and I quipped, "Oh, you're late! Do you think you're pregnant? Why don't you take advantage that we are at a grocery store and buy a pregnancy test?"

Richelle sarcastically replied, "Are you seriously asking me to take a pregnancy test here at Publix?"

I coolly said, "Yes, why not?"

Richelle relented and purchased the pregnancy test (two actually) and went to the bathroom to take them. The few minutes that it took her to take the pregnancy tests felt like an eternity. I had all sorts of thoughts running through my head. *Was I really going to be a dad? What kind of father would I be? What if this is a false alarm and I'm getting excited over nothing?* She finally ran out of the bathroom, crying hysterically, and told me, "Babe, we're pregnant!"

I began crying tears of joy and hollering, "We're pregnant! We are having a baby!" right in the middle of the grocery store. People began noticing the commotion and must have thought that we had gone crazy. We were so ecstatic to be parents. Richelle and I were hugging and kissing each other, and after we realized the stir that we caused, we quietly left the store and called our parents to inform them that they would soon become grandparents. They were thrilled and excited for us, especially since Adrian—our first-born—would be the first grandchild on both sides of our family.

Afterward, we finally got to our apartment, and as we stepped in, Richelle informed me, "Will, now that I'm pregnant, I don't think this condo will suit us. After a year living here, we should move back to the suburbs of Weston to begin our life as a family."

I was stunned! I was so excited to live on the beach, as it had always been my dream, so I insisted that we should continue living at the beach to no avail. Richelle was not having any of it. I finally relented and realized that she was right. It is difficult to live in a condo with a newborn. I also wanted to make her happy. As they say, "Happy wife, happy life," so after our one-year lease was up in October 2011, we decided to move back in with Richelle's parents to save money since I was opening my dental practice. But, I do not want to get too ahead of myself.

I will now let Richelle share her horror story of being a pharmacy manager at an underperforming pharmacy that was being terrorized by two toxic technicians all while being pregnant with our son, Adrian.

Chapter Six

Turning the Ship Around

Richelle Peña

Pᴿᴵᴼᴿ ᴛᴼ ʟᴇᴀᴠɪɴɢ Cᴀʟɪꜰᴏʀɴɪᴀ, I told my manager that I was moving back home. He was disappointed that I was leaving because he had designated me as "high potential," which meant that I was on track to climb the rungs of the corporate ladder at Target Corporation.

He nonetheless transferred me to a store in the city of North Miami and recommended to his counterpart in Florida that I retain my title of "pharmacy manager." I was happy that I found a job in my hometown and I was able to retain my rank and salary, but little did I know that I would be the manager of a pharmacy that was not doing well financially and also had some serious issues with the staff. This particular pharmacy had a slew of issues ranging from lagging sales, problematic interns, and not surprisingly, customer service issues. This assignment was not meant to be a punishment, but rather an opportunity for me and the store to succeed, since I had a history of turning stores like this one around.

The North Miami store that I was assigned to was a bit far for me, but my new manager explained that if I was able to turn around this particular store, I would then be transferred to a store closer to home and, shortly after, I would be promoted to a regional pharmacy manager position. I was excited by this prospect and took on the arduous task of turning around the faltering pharmacy.

This assignment would prove to be a challenge, even for me. This particular store was one of the worst in the district. Even though I had done this type of work before, I was intimidated by my newfound reality. There were high expectations of me, as I was brought in as the "white knight" to salvage a lagging and underperforming pharmacy. I knew that I needed to turn around the store and fast. As I mentioned, sales were faltering, my team lacked camaraderie, and our customer service scores were trending negative. I had two pharmacy team members that apparently had been given too much slack by prior management and were used to doing things their way. When I came into the store, they immediately saw me as an existential threat since I was brought in "to clean house." They immediately began trying to exert their dominance over me, telling me how the pharmacy ought to be run, what the customers were like, etc. I thanked them for their unsolicited advice, and I began doing my own assessment of the pharmacy and its operations. The two technicians continued to badger me and disrespect my rank as their leader.

At the beginning, I would come home crying to Will, and he would sit down with me and ask me what had transpired at the pharmacy during the day. I told him that I hated my job and felt disrespected by my two pharmacy technicians that I worked with. I continued my tirade, saying that my team members in California were so different, that we were a high-functioning team and we all got along. I told him that my new team members were rude to me and our patients, and would often give me the "silent treatment," where not one word would be uttered to me all day. I was uncomfortable, and rightfully so.

Will said, "You feel uncomfortable at the moment because you are being faced with a challenge that you didn't experience before. When working at your store in California, you inherited a high-performing store. Now you are being given a store with lackluster performance and asked to turn it into a high-performing pharmacy, but you have problematic team members." He continued, "Have you sat down with these two individuals and had a candid conversation with them about their performance?"

I had not. Honestly, I had no idea how to have critical conversations with employees since I never had to do them in my previous post.

Will advised me to confront the issue immediately rather than continue avoiding it, because animosity was building on both sides, which was obviously not good. He told me that ultimately the technicians and I needed to find common ground where we could collaborate and successfully get our jobs done. Our patients relied on us to be accurate and efficient, and if we were not because of our own internal strife, then patients would unnecessarily have to wait for their much-needed medicines, or worse, they would get the wrong prescription (which could have negative and even fatal consequences).

Around this time (circa November 2010), I found out I was pregnant with Adrian. I was exhilarated about being pregnant and one day being a mom. I was also having some nausea, since I was in my first trimester of pregnancy. Needless to say, I was at my wit's end with the situation at my pharmacy, and being pregnant with raging hormones did not help ameliorate the situation!

Yet, I dug in my heels and continued complaining. I thought about those two individuals even while I tried to sleep. I was not used to confrontation and just wanted everyone to get along and do their job. As the night wore on, however, I thought over what Will had told me and realized that he was right—I needed to speak to the technicians as soon as possible.

The next day at work, I spoke to my human resource (HR) manager and explained the situation that I was having with my technicians. To my surprise, he told me that those two individuals had been a menace to the other pharmacists that worked at my pharmacy before I did, and they were the reason why so many pharmacists had left their job or quit pharmacy altogether. I was shocked by this revelation! I knew I had a real problem on my hands and asked my manager for advice.

He said, "We have to follow the proper protocols. You first need to sit down with these individuals, explain the situation, and tell them that the conversation is being documented. If they still do not demonstrate any positive change after speaking with them and providing warnings, then we can think about termination, but before then you need to speak with them and have proper documentation."

I left his office obfuscated and nervous. I had to confront two employees that had caused so much misery to my predecessors. I returned to the pharmacy and decided that I needed to take charge— not to exert dominance or be condescending, but to inform these individuals that they needed to get with the program or else we would have to part ways. I sat down with one of the technicians and explained my stance. I told her that I was the leader of the pharmacy tasked with turning around the operations and that I needed her help in order to accomplish my turnaround efforts. She looked at me like I had cursed her unborn child and simply said, "Pfff . . . whatever!" then proceeded to walk out on me!

The other technician had a similar reaction when I spoke to her on a separate occasion, but at least she seemed a bit more receptive to my request. However, during work they both continued with their notoriously poor behavior. They continued showing up late for work, providing poor customer service to our patients, and giving me attitude whenever they were in a bad mood.

I began practicing some introspection, thinking, *Perhaps I am the problem. Many books state that employees do not leave bad jobs; they leave bad bosses.* I continued my efforts to have these individuals buy into my turnaround plan, speaking to them on numerous occasions to no avail. I tried killing them with kindness, which also did not work. They continued with their negative attitude, and finally, I was fed up. I went from being shy and intimidated to being assertive and taking charge. I knew that as much as I wanted to inspire these individuals to do better, they were fixated on not wanting to change or heed my numerous warnings regarding their job performance. It was a lost cause—nothing that I did was going to change the poor attitudes of these individuals.

My plan was to ultimately terminate both of these toxic individuals from my pharmacy, but I needed to be methodical in my approach. If I fired both technicians at the same time, I would be left with the entire workload of the pharmacy to myself. I decided to terminate the worst-performing technician first (the one that dismissed my plight to turn around the pharmacy offhandedly and walked out on me), while I worked on a transition plan for the second technician.

As my next step, I spoke to HR and got all the requisite documentation ready. When I finally received the approval to proceed with termination from my HR director, I planned a date to part ways with the first individual.

I am not going to say that I wasn't nervous. After all, it was my first time terminating another individual, and I was unsure how she was going to take the news. *Was she going to simply acknowledge her own faults and leave amicably? Would she recognize that she did not correct her behavior on time and admit her mistakes? Or was she going to blow up on me and accuse me of wrongful termination?* The decision to part ways with this individual weighed heavily on me. There was not a moment throughout the day that I did not ruminate on the task that loomed in the not so distant future. Thankfully, HR was available to coach and guide me on how to properly deliver the message. The HR director told me, "Richelle, you have had numerous coaching sessions with this individual. There should be no surprises when you tell her that you have tried to work with her, but she has not responded accordingly to your suggestions or feedback."

Intuitively, I knew that this conversation should not catch her off guard, but I was still nervous about actually sitting down and having to let go of an individual that had been with the company for so many years.

I finally worked up the courage to bring my technician into the office and have the dreaded conversation. I had someone from the HR department sit in the meeting as a witness, and I began my rehearsed speech. To be honest, the specifics of the conversation elude me, as I was so nervous about the whole ordeal. I simply stuck with the facts and delivered the message with as much empathy as I possibly could.

In the end, the individual understood, nodded in acknowledgment, and simply stood up and left the office without even thanking us for the opportunity to work at our pharmacy. I was slightly disappointed by her reaction, but I was also relieved that it was over and that this employee was no longer my responsibility.

Once I parted ways with her, the second technician realized I was no longer going to put up with her poor performance. Her performance improved temporarily, but after some time, her attitude continued to be an issue, and she was eventually let go.

After each of these toxic individuals left, I hired new technicians. I made sure to hire team members that were collaborative and had a great attitude with patients. As I had learned in Target Business College, I used situational based questions to gain insight on the personalities and thought processes of these new individuals. Admittedly, the difference the new technicians made in the pharmacy was remarkable. It was a breath of fresh air. Patient wait times were down, satisfaction scores were up, and our key performance metrics were finally trending positive. I had finally turned an underperforming store into a high performer simply by letting go of my two unmotivated and problematic technicians and replacing them with individuals that were self-motivated and responsible.

Personally, I learned a lot from this experience. I learned that you need to get in front of your problems, resolve them quickly, and not let them fester. If you fail to address problems in a timely manner, a small problem will soon become a bigger issue and will be harder to deal with. Admittedly, having critical conversations with your employees regarding their performance is downright difficult, but it is an essential—and necessary—skill as a manager or leader.

Secondly, I learned that there will be people on your team that you unfortunately cannot lead and inspire. That's okay. You cannot take it personally or take it as a defeat. Sometimes you inadvertently hire people with a poor attitude or negative demeanor. Recognize who they are and address them immediately. From experience, I have learned that a disgruntled employee will eventually spoil the rest of the team.

The nightmarish experience with my technicians was emotionally draining for me, but I was fortunate to be able to use my HR director as a resource during this whole ordeal. I was also grateful to be able to lean on Will and ask him for advice on what to do with my team members at work. The fact that I was able to talk about my issues with my husband was extremely comforting. Will was my shoulder to cry on when I felt helpless about my situation at the pharmacy. This seemingly negative experience also taught us as a married couple to rely on one another when we faced challenges or difficult situations. This helped us tremendously throughout our professional careers. When the road got dark and treacherous, at least we knew we had each other and were not alone on the journey.

After that, my pharmacy was finally performing well. I had accomplished the seemingly impossible task of turning around the operations, and my pharmacy was now profitable, with remarkable customer service scores. I was proud of my accomplishments, but now that the challenge was eliminated, I was bored simply being a pharmacist. Even though I love helping people, I loathed having to stand behind a counter for hours dispensing medicines. I realized that I had pursued a career in pharmacy to appease my parents, but as an extrovert, I felt that my profession was a mismatch for my personality.

For starters, I needed to remain laser-focused on my tasks to ensure that I was dispensing the correct medicine with the accurate dosage for the right patient. An error on my part could be putting someone else's life in jeopardy, and I took this responsibility very seriously. Furthermore, I enjoyed counseling my patients, but I needed to keep my conversations to a minimum because I had other prescriptions that needed to be filled. I was also working evenings and weekends, which meant I missed a lot of important family gatherings and dinners with Will. Since I was also pregnant, my feet would swell and ache from standing all day long. To say that I was miserable working at the pharmacy would be an understatement. These factors also made me realize that although I was grateful to be a pharmacist, I knew it was not going to be my long-term goal.

I also grew disenchanted with corporate culture and all the bureaucratic red tape that I needed to traverse to get anything accomplished. For example, it took me several months to finally terminate two individuals that were known to be problematic. They had caused so many pharmacists before me to either quit or transfer pharmacies. Even though they were a menace, and I eventually gathered all the necessary documentation to terminate them, the legal and HR departments initially could not agree on a timeline for when to terminate these individuals. Meanwhile, I was carrying the brunt of trying to manage a dysfunctional pharmacy while working alongside two vile individuals. I was also being pressured by my superiors to meet revenue expectations, control our expenses, enforce our policies and procedures, provide exceptional customer service, etc.

For all these reasons, I eventually burned out and began strongly reconsidering my original plans of climbing the corporate ladder. I kept thinking to myself, *Is this really the life I want to have, where it's all about dollars and cents? With the immense pressure that corporate leaders operate with, will I be able to be a mom and wife? Will I be able to spend quality time with my kids and still conduct my managerial duties?*

Despite my apprehensions about remaining a pharmacist and ascending the corporate hierarchy, I did not know what else to do with my pharmacy degree. *Should I look for another job elsewhere?* I knew that I did not want to work at another pharmacy because my friends who worked in other retail pharmacy chains complained about their horrible work conditions all the time. I felt stuck and did not know what to do. I thought of leaving the pharmacy world behind and joining Will on his new business venture, but at the time, the office was still in the design phase and had not yet opened. We also could not afford for me to leave the pharmacy since we were financially tethered to my job.

The thoughts, nonetheless, began crossing my mind, *Could we possibly join forces one day and work together? How would it be working with my husband? Is working with Will and building a business the right move for me and my family?* There were many questions and even more unknown answers. In the interim, I knew for certain that I wanted my professional career to head in a different direction.

Chapter Seven

Difficult Decisions

William Peña

Duringthe initial stages of planning my first dental practice in late 2010, Richelle remained employed at the pharmacy in North Miami. She was figuring out how to turn around her pharmacy's operations and was dealing with the two underperforming and disrespectful individuals who were making her miserable. Although she had her hands full with her pharmacy duties, and had to deal with the aches and pains of being pregnant, she was still involved in the design and planning of my first dental practice. At this stage, she did not openly express an interest in working with me since she was dealing with contentious issues at work, and the reality was we could not afford to have both of us work in a startup practice making no money. We were penny-pinching our way to business success and still relied heavily on Richelle's salary. Nevertheless, I leaned on her for her opinions on office location, interior design, marketing, etc. Even though we were not officially business partners at this stage, we still acted as though we were. Richelle has always been invested in my projects and my dreams, and I, too, am supportive and invested in her goals.

Richelle suggested that we build an office in a middle-to-high-class neighborhood in a heavily transited intersection since these areas have high numbers of children (our target demographic). Since we are both south Florida natives, we know the neighborhoods and relied on our own intuition to select a locale. We also relied on stats we gathered on the internet (Wikipedia was a great aid) to help us identify areas with high concentrations of young families with children.

We eventually found a nice corner property that met our search criteria in a suburb known as Pembroke Pines. As I mentioned before, I knew the area well because I lived in this city when I attended high school. We hired a sales rep from a dental supply company to help us equip the office, and along with the architect and general contractor, we worked together in designing our flagship practice.

For the first office, I decided to go big. So big, in fact, that our equipment rep tried to talk me out of building such a large practice. He was concerned that I was going to spend a lot of money equipping such an enormous space, and he was also worried that there were a lot of competitors in the surrounding area. I was unmoved by his concerns because I had previously done my homework and knew who our so-called competitors were. None of those offices were going to offer the services I offered, nor were they accepting patients with Medicaid. I intuitively knew that my business model would rely heavily on high patient volume, and for that we needed a big enough office space.

I thanked the rep for his concern and proceeded, undeterred, with my original plan. I did, however, recognize the size and scope of the project and did not want to get overly confident in my projections. After consulting with Richelle, we decided that if we were going to go big with our first office, then we needed to balance our ambitions by being prudent and fiscally responsible with our personal finances.

We had already made the decision when Richelle found out she was pregnant with Adrian that when the lease expired, we would move out of our beautiful waterfront condo in Sunny Isles Beach and move back in with her parents in the suburbs. This would help us save money on rent. Although I was bummed at the prospect of leaving behind my luxury beachside lifestyle, I also knew that I needed to be a responsible parent and entrepreneur.

At the end of June of 2011, Richelle began having contractions. This was unexpected since it was a week earlier than her expected delivery date. I immediately rushed her to the hospital, and she was admitted. After many hours of experiencing contractions, the doctor determined that she had what is known as "failure to progress," and she had to undergo a cesarean section. I was in the operating room with her, holding her hand. I was both excited and nervous to meet my son for the first time, but I was also concerned for Richelle, who was tired and experiencing a great deal of discomfort. It is in those crucial moments that you realize how special being a mother really is. Our obstetrician delivered our son and, after cleaning him, placed my little boy in my arms.

Words cannot describe the rush of emotions I felt when I held my son, Adrian, for the first time. It was literally love at first sight! He was so little and vulnerable, and I wanted nothing more than to protect him and keep him in my arms. I kissed his little forehead and said a prayer over him. I was now a father, and it honestly felt amazing.

I always say that my wedding night and the days my children were born are the most memorable moments of my life, and my greatest joy, to date, has been becoming a husband and father.

As I held Adrian, and with tears flowing from my eyes, I promised my son that I would always be present in his life, and that I would always guide and protect him. While holding my son for the first time as a new parent, the flow of emotions running through me made me realize how precious life is. It also made me realize that as much as I needed to be a provider in the financial sense, my priority would always be to be present in the lives of my children and witness them blossom into adults. I am not sure what made me enter into this sort of trance, but I kept promising myself and Adrian that I would always be present for him and that I would continue to love and protect his mother.

In retrospect, it was probably because my dad had sacrificed so much when I was a child to search for better economic opportunities in a new country. He had to leave me when I was a newborn, and I would not see him again until I was four years old. Perhaps this subconsciously made me yearn to be more present in the lives of my children.

Witnessing Adrian's birth made me think of how I would handle being a new business owner and a new parent. The office was opening up in a few months and I was concerned that it would be so time-consuming, that I would have little or no time to spend with my baby boy. I knew that I did not want to be a workaholic father and miss seeing my child grow up. Understandably I needed to be responsible and dedicate time to grow the practice, but I would not allow it to control nor take over my life. I was unsure of how I was going to manage it all, but at that point, I made a conscious decision to always be present at home with my family.

Chapter Eight

Evolution

Richelle Peña

IN JUNE OF 2011, my beautiful baby boy, Adrian, came into the world. Will and I were so grateful and happy to be new parents. Becoming a mother made me further realize that I needed a career change. It had always been my priority to be present in the lives of my children, and working a corporate job was not conducive to fulfilling my personal goals.

I had not yet decided what my next career move would be, but in the interim I decided to help Will build up his practice since he had no marketing experience. I was honestly as excited as he was about the new office and I wanted to be a part of it from day one.

Prior to opening our office, I created a business Facebook and Twitter account and began creating ads. I also recruited my friend, Stephanie, who had experience working in public relations, to help us create our first promotional videos which we then posted on our company's new YouTube page. I did all this while being sleep-deprived and taking care of a newborn at home.

Fortunately, Will has always been a team player, and he, too, has always been present in the lives of our children. He would stay up throughout the night feeding Adrian and changing his soiled diapers just so I could snatch a few hours of much-needed sleep. Seeing him somnolent from taking care of Adrian throughout the night as he went off to work in the morning made me realize that Will was the kind of person that was committed wholeheartedly to his family, and as a new mom, this gave me a lot of reassurance.

I was enjoying my time working alongside my husband and helping him market the office and planning for the opening. There were moments when I caught myself daydreaming of the possibility of one day joining forces with Will and feeling a little tingly at the thought of building a business with him. But as soon as those thoughts popped into my head, I would readily dismiss them. As I had previously mentioned, we could not afford to work together.

Which is why I was so surprised when Will approached me while I was still on maternity leave and asked me, "What do you think of the possibility of quitting your pharmacy job and helping me build the business?"

He caught me completely off guard and after regaining my composure and realizing what he had just said, I asked him with a concerned, but slightly excited tone, "What do you mean? Do you think that's a good idea? Don't you think I should stay working at the pharmacy to help us bankroll the office? We don't know how this office will perform, and we should not take any chances."

Will responded, "You are absolutely correct, *but* I need help training the front desk team. I have no idea how to do the patient scheduling, insurance verification, or payment collection. I know the clinical aspect of the business, and I figured out how to finance and actually build the office, but now I need help with staff training and the administrative stuff."

Nervously, I responded, "Will, we are taking a huge risk. This is a big ask. You and I are basically jumping into the deep end of the pool here with no life vest. You are asking me to quit my job when you don't have a job, and now you are asking me to build this business with you? You do realize that we rely on the business scaling quickly enough before our money runs out. If we don't succeed, it's literally game over for us."

We had working capital in the bank that would cover approximately three months' worth of expenses. We had also invested all of our personal savings into this new business venture. We were starting an office with no patients in the middle of the suburbs with over thirteen pediatric dentists in a three-mile radius, and my unemployed husband was asking me to quit my six-figure-salary job to join his startup. I thought he had lost his mind.

I asked him again, this time with a hint of acerbity in my voice, "How exactly do you plan on keeping us afloat? We have a newborn son, and we already live with my parents. There is literally no other expense we can cut if this plan of yours backfires!"

Then he proceeded to drop the gauntlet, "Can you withdraw your retirement savings in your 401(k)? It would give us an extra few months of runway so we could hustle and get the business up and running. With your help and my clinical skills we could be a dynamite team! What do you say?"

Honestly, I did not know what to say. For a while, I remained speechless.

Sensing my apprehension, Will attempted to reassure me by telling me, "Listen, I know you are worried and upset, but I have a plan. It's a calculated risk, but the truth is, I really need your help and expertise. You have corporate experience working at Target, and we could really use it. Besides, we will be working together to build an incredible business that will help thousands of families in the community."

I thought about Will's proposal for a moment. This decision would involve me sacrificing a secure salary and venturing out into the risky world of business and entrepreneurship. If things worked out well, I would not have to work at the pharmacy any longer, I could have a more flexible schedule, I could be present in the life of my son and future children, and I could possibly one day be financially independent.

However, if things didn't go according to plan, then Will and I would both face financial ruin. It was a calculated risk, and I'd be lying if I said it didn't make me nervous and extremely apprehensive, but I strongly believed in his vision of creating a business to help underserved children. I also saw the immense opportunity to create a successful business around this vision.

Furthermore, we acknowledged that in the event of the business not succeeding, both Will and I would have no trouble securing positions in our respective fields. This is primarily due to the healthcare industry's unwavering stability and high demand. This was not ideal, but at least it was an option.

After processing Will's proposal and weighing out all the options, I looked Will in the eye and told him bluntly, "Hell yes! Let's do this together." I was tired of working at the pharmacy and fed up with all the corporate nonsense. I wanted to strike out on my own, with my husband, and build something meaningful together. I wanted us to make decisions that were in alignment with our company's vision and our own values.

To be honest, I was scared, or more aptly, straight up terrified of venturing into the unknown, but at least I knew that Will and I were in this together. I intuitively knew that Will and I would make a phenomenal team at both work and with our family, since we had already proven to each other that we were always willing to invest the necessary time and energy into making our marriage a success. Now that we had a baby, I saw how Will was committed to being an active participant in raising our children. I knew that managing and growing a business would be no different. We would face issues and obstacles together, and as a team, we would climb to the pinnacle of our success.

I would love to tell you that it was smooth sailing and happy days from that day forth. Little did I know the crazy roller-coaster ride that awaited us. This scary thrill ride had numerous ups and downs, and there were terrifying moments when all I saw was darkness. It was one of the scariest things I have done in my life. It shook Will and me to the core. It even tested our faith. I knew, however, that if we stuck together, we would eventually see the light of day. And eventually, we did, but that's a story for another chapter.

For now, we knew that we were on this journey together, as partners in marriage and also in business. It was both exhilarating and frightening at the same time.

I then asked Will, "I know your heart is in the right place, and, trust me, I am invested in this venture with you and I trust you completely, but I am curious about one thing. With all the pediatric dental offices near us, why don't they accept Medicaid or see patients with special needs, as you are wanting to do? What do you know that they don't?"

Will then confidently responded, "Great question. I did my homework. I researched the majority of pediatric dentists in our county and the neighboring ones. None of those dentists accept Medicaid, or at least it is not listed as an insurance plan they accept on their websites. I also spoke to the Medicaid representatives, and they mentioned that they have thousands of members but have no dental office to refer them to since barely any dentists in south Florida accept it. They were actually thrilled about our business model!"

Regarding patients with special needs, Will explained, "From my experience working in private practice and at the residency programs both here in Florida and in San Francisco, I witnessed firsthand how the university was really the only place where patients with special needs could turn to for dental care. I was told by my professors and colleagues at the university that pediatric dentists in private practice are apprehensive about treating the special needs community because oftentimes these patients do not have the behavioral maturity to sit for an exam and, much less, to allow treatment. According to these dentists, patients with special needs would require sedation or general anesthesia to treat, and they frankly do not have the necessary permits nor the access to a hospital to perform these procedures."

Will's confidence put me at ease. He had clearly done his research, and the information he obtained confirmed his theory of there being a real lack of dentists accepting Medicaid and accepting patients with special needs at their practice. But I still wondered, how would we make money if the reimbursements from Medicaid were so low?

I will let Will answer this important question in the next chapter.

Chapter Nine

Setting the Vision

William Peña

I WAS THRILLED THAT RICHELLE had decided to embark on this business journey with me. It was a relief to know that my wife, whom I genuinely trust and admire, was going to help me build our company. Her corporate background would prove invaluable to our venture, providing expertise in areas such as recruitment, marketing, and training. More importantly, my wife is an excellent communicator and adept at cultivating relationships, which would be useful for the interpersonal aspects of our business. Our complementary skill sets and personalities would undoubtedly be of tremendous value to our new venture.

Although Richelle was committed to the idea of us working together to build our company, she wanted reassurance as to exactly how we intended to make the business model work. After all, she did have a point. Medicaid participation by dentists in Florida was low, and there had to be a reason. At one point, I also had the same skepticism, but rather than dismiss the idea altogether, I dug into the issue a bit deeper and analyzed the data myself. If there was a way that I could pursue my altruistic goal and also create a profitable business

49

that was scalable (the goal was to own several offices, not just one), then I was going to move forward with my plan.

I already had a glimpse of how a Medicaid practice ran while working with my first employer. I recognized that perhaps my first private practice experience was not the best example of how an office that accepted Medicaid should be structured. After all, that office ran chaotically and haphazardly. But at least I knew that there was strong demand from patients and I decided to learn from those negative experiences to make our own office better.

I researched other pediatric dental offices within a five-mile radius of our practice. I looked at their social media pages and their websites, and read their online reviews. I even read the doctors' bios and their stated mission statement, but frankly none of these other offices really had anything that stood out to me as unique. Furthermore, based on my extensive online sleuthing, I noticed that none of those pediatric dental offices accepted the insurance plans we planned to accept, for example, Medicaid (which was a huge unmet need); none offered advanced treatment modalities such as sedation and hospital dentistry (which I was credentialed for); and none were open at opportune times for parents (evenings and on weekends). This would give us a head start and provide a competitive advantage.

As Richelle mentioned earlier, one of the issues when dealing with Medicaid, and a main reason why participation in the Medicaid program in Florida is so low (at least back in 2011 when we opened our first practice), is the low reimbursements dentists receive for services rendered. Usually a pediatric dental office accepting Medicaid would have to see about twice the number of patients to make the same amount of money as an office that solely accepts private insurance. To see this many patients, an office would also need to hire more staff—more dental assistants and front desk personnel—to be able to handle this increased patient load.

Since industry benchmarks for a thriving pediatric dental practice are well-known, I used them to reverse-engineer the number of patients we needed to see on a daily basis in order to meet our intended annual financial targets. Based on my calculations, I determined that we needed to see approximately forty to fifty patients each work day. This was also in alignment with the number of patients I saw at my first job and I felt comfortable handling this patient load. Granted, I would have to see more patients daily than a typical office accepting patients with private insurance, but at least I was reassured by the fact that I was meeting a real need in the community.

I explained all of this to Richelle, walking her through the arithmetic. If she had been onboard with the idea of working together before, my due diligence further cemented her decision. She mentioned that it was great seeing how our large, overarching financial objectives were broken down into smaller, feasible daily goals. This clarity, in turn, really drove our confidence in our business.

Now that Richelle and I were officially business partners we sat down prior to opening our office and delineated our leadership approach. Since we are both generous and collaborative individuals, we knew that we wanted to foster a work environment where all team members felt comfortable enough to share their ideas and provide suggestions. We wanted to support our team and encourage them to do the right thing for our patients. There would be no reproach or chastisement on our part. Our goal was to hire individuals that took initiative and were self-motivated, that were eager to grow with our company and felt empowered by our company's guiding principles (more on this in ensuing chapters).

We also determined that I should lead the business as CEO since I am a pediatric dentist and I had initially set the vision for the company. Richelle determined that she would focus on hiring new team members, establishing front-desk processes, and marketing the practice. We agreed to respect one another and that there would be no power struggle between us.

Now, if you choose to embark on the entrepreneurial journey with a spouse or partner, it is vital to establish clear roles and responsibilities right from the start. Consider each other's strengths and weaknesses, and determine which positions within the company can best leverage your respective talents and skill sets. Define your leadership roles and make an agreement to respect each other's authority and boundaries. Failure to adhere to this simple rule can lead to conflicts, resentment, and frustration.

Creating the desired culture within your business is the next step when setting up a venture with your spouse. Culture encompasses shared values, attitudes, and behaviors that shape the work environment. As founders, you have the power to influence the type of culture you want to cultivate. Decide whether you aim for a collaborative team culture or one centered around exceptional customer service; or both, as it was in our case.

If you find yourself unsure of where to start, fear not! In the next chapter, Richelle will provide effective guidance on shaping your company's culture based on a shared set of beliefs and guiding principles.

Chapter Ten

Creating a Company Culture

Richelle Peña

WITH OUR ROLES AND responsibilities clearly delineated, we now needed to set expectations for our team based on our shared vision as founders of the company. Will and I knew that by delineating our expectations for our team, we would ultimately shape our company's culture. We therefore took our time to craft a list of guiding principles which we called our *Credo*, and it consisted of the following nineteen principles:

1. Have a positive mindset—no skunks allowed!

2. Be open to change—we are constantly evolving.

3. There is no such thing as a lapse in integrity.

4. "Team first" mentality—our patients come second.

5. Open and honest communication—be a one-minute manager.

6. No one is as good as all of us.

7. We are not a tooth business; we are a *people* business.

8. Be humble and approachable.

9. Hire for attitude; train for skill.

10. Be accessible to the community.

11. Provide a "wow experience" to all our guests.

12. Nothing is impossible.

13. Have serious fun—smile always!

14. We celebrate mistakes—learn and grow.

15. We offer autonomy, but expect accountability.

16. Get comfortable being uncomfortable—life begins outside your comfort zone.

17. Take initiative—if there is a problem, offer a solution.

18. Trust, but verify.

19. Always, always do what is right for the patient!

We understood that our Credo would serve as a compass for our team, guiding their actions and decisions in alignment with our company's vision and mission. It was important for us to create a culture that emphasized trust, transparency, and accountability, and our Credo would play a crucial role in achieving that. Each principle in our Credo was carefully thought out and reflected our core values.

Integrity was at the forefront, as we believed in conducting business with honesty and ethical practices. We wanted our team to prioritize doing the right thing, even when faced with difficult choices.

Continuous improvement was another key value for us. We recognized that growth and progress were essential for the success of our company. We urged our team to embrace a mindset of learning and development, constantly seeking ways to enhance their skills and knowledge.

Collaboration was a fundamental principle that we highlighted in our Credo. We firmly believed that the collective efforts of a team could achieve far more than individual contributions. We encouraged open communication, active listening, and the sharing of ideas to create an environment where everyone's input is valued.

Compassion was a value close to our hearts. Will and I believed that by prioritizing empathy and kindness, we could build strong relationships within our team and promote a sense of belonging.

Once our Credo was finalized, we shared it with our team, explaining the rationale behind each principle and how it aligned with our company's vision. We encouraged them to internalize these values and integrate them into their daily work.

To ensure that our Credo was not just a document gathering dust, we incorporated it into our hiring process, performance evaluations, and every decision-making. We wanted every member of our team to understand and embrace our shared values, and to know that they were being held accountable for upholding them.

Over time, we witnessed the positive impact of our Credo on our company's culture. It became the foundation for how we operated, guiding our actions, and shaping our interactions.

As founders, we were proud to have created a company culture that was rooted in our shared values and beliefs. Our Credo served as a constant reminder of who we were as a company and what we aspired to achieve. It was a testament to our commitment to building a successful and ethical business that made a positive difference in the world.

Now that you understand the basis of our guiding principles, I will dig deeper on how these principles originated and how we actually utilized them at work (and even in our own personal lives).

Have a positive mindset—no skunks allowed!

Will and I believe that positivity is a critical factor in achieving happiness and productivity. When establishing our company culture, we took a proactive approach in recruiting team members who possessed a positive mindset. Negative individuals tend to focus on complaints and always seem to find problems rather than solutions. Just like a rotten apple, these negative individuals have the potential to spoil the entire team. In the event that we hired someone who later exhibited a negative attitude, we made efforts to uplift and support them. However, if it became clear that their negativity persisted, we made the decision to swiftly remove them from our team. At our company, we prioritized a careful and thorough hiring process, but we were also decisive in letting go individuals who brought a negative attitude to the workplace. Retaining individuals with a negative mindset not only diminished the overall morale of the team, but also undermined and sabotaged our collective efforts.

No skunks allowed was added to the positive mindset principle because we asked all or our team members to leave their personal issues at home. A "skunk" referred to someone who "stinks" up the office. Similar to a negative mindset/attitude, carrying personal burdens into the office would drag down productivity and kill the mood of the team.

Be open to change—we are constantly evolving.

This guiding principle required our team to be adaptable. If there was a way that we could do something better, we wanted to know about it. Many of the most important changes made in the company arose from the feedback and suggestions of our team members. We made it a habit to proactively ask our team for ways to improve our business, and went as far as asking our team members which processes and protocols they considered ineffective, or downright absurd, that were inhibiting them from properly performing their jobs. We weighed the merits of every idea given to us—even the craziest ones—as long as they were grounded and related to the issue at hand.

As an example, we implemented a protocol that dental assistants—and not the front desk team—were responsible for scheduling follow-up appointments since this was creating a bottleneck upon checkout. This alleviated the crowding of people at the checkout counter, and patients' experiences improved by shortening their time at the office.

On other occasions, the changes we made in the company arose from our own personal experiences. An example of this came about when I found out I was pregnant with Adrian. On our very first appointment to our obstetrician's office, Will and I were taken to her personal office. I was shocked because normally when you visit a physician's office, they bring you into a cold, sterile room with an examination chair. But our obstetrician's process was different. She actually took the time to talk with us in her own personal office. She started by congratulating us on being first-time parents (which I found to be an especially warm, empathetic touch) and later proceeded to explain what I should expect throughout the different stages of my pregnancy.

From this delightful experience with my obstetrician, I decided to implement something similar at our office. We called it the "patient intake process" and it served many purposes. The first was to welcome, build rapport, and create a connection with our new patients. The second was for us to find out how our patients had heard about our office. Lastly, we took the opportunity during the intake process to go over our policies and to have patients sign the requisite consents.

There is no such thing as a lapse in integrity.

Although many people correctly use the terms honesty and integrity interchangeably, we specifically refer to integrity as doing the right thing even if no one is watching. Both Will and I have an intolerance toward dishonest and sneaky individuals, and we did not want anyone on our team that lacked a proper code of ethics. If we encountered a team member exhibiting this sort of improper behavior, they would immediately be terminated.

"Team first" mentality—our patients come second.

We intuitively knew that if we put our team members first, then our patients would, in turn, be taken care of. We made it a point to properly take care of our team by creating an environment where ideas could be safely shared, and we took the time to properly teach team members whenever a mistake occurred rather than simply scolding them. A team that felt appreciated and heard would, in turn, be happier and more productive at work, and patients would benefit by having a great experience.

When Will and I go to a business where we see a disgruntled or unhappy employee, our initial thought is that the individual does not feel valued or appreciated. Rather than blame the employee for their poor behavior, we hold management responsible. Ultimately, having a toxic team culture will affect the team's energy, and it will eventually drive customers away.

If the leader is a tyrant—like my first boss at the pharmacy—and he or she does not provide positive feedback and belittles his or her team members, then they will eventually become disgruntled and leave the company—or, worse, they will stay and take out their frustrations on the customers.

Remember, employees do not leave bad jobs; they leave bad bosses.

Open and honest communication—be a one-minute manager.

One of my favorite management books is *The One Minute Manager* by Ken Blanchard and Spencer Johnson. This short but powerful book describes how effective managers take a brief moment—one minute or less—to set goals, praise good work, and address problems with their team members. This book, in my opinion, is so impactful in its simple approach to communicating with your team members that it was required reading for any new manager starting at our business.

After reading this book and going through my leadership training (which was based on the principles explained in *The One Minute Manager*), managers were expected to have open and honest dialogue with their direct reports. Problems needed to be addressed immediately, and we encouraged our office managers to catch their team members doing something good and celebrate their wins with the rest of the team.

No one is as good as all of us.

As is the common thread in this book thus far, Will and I have a team approach to everything we do. From raising our kids, to planning events with friends, and in business, we foster a sense of camaraderie. We truly believe if you have the right people on your team, you can create synergy where no individual on that team is stronger than the team as a whole.

This is why it was so important for us to hire great team members that aligned with our company's vision. If we were able to build a team with rock-star individuals that had a desire to help and serve those less fortunate, then we knew we could create a great culture at our company.

We are not a tooth business; we are a **people** *business.*

Our team made every patient feel welcomed regardless of their insurance plan. At other offices, patients are treated and scheduled according to the type of insurance plan they have. The better the plan, the better the level of service. Both Will and I frowned on this type of behavior. It was the antithesis of the company culture we were trying to create. Will and I wanted every patient—regardless of insurance plan, race, medical condition, etc.—to be treated with respect, love, and dignity. This was our objective. To this day, we want every single person that comes to any of our offices to leave with a positive impression of the dentist and the team, and most importantly, we want our patients to look forward to coming to their appointments.

We viewed every interaction with patients as an experience and not simply a transaction. When a patient was nervous or apprehensive, our team would sing and, at times, even dance in an attempt to distract or appease them. We did anything it took for our young patients to feel welcomed and, most importantly, loved and appreciated.

Be humble and approachable.

When I was a pharmacy intern, I had a boss that was unapproachable. His leadership style was to use intimidation to get his team to do what needed to get done—similar to a tyrant. If I made a mistake, he would ridicule me in front of the team. He had poor communication skills and lacked interpersonal connections with team members. I dreaded going to work and counted down the days when I would be able to transfer to a new store. In part because of this experience, Will and I made it a mandate for all the leaders in the company—whether they were a doctor, an office manager, or administrator—to be humble and approachable. If they lacked this sort of character, we would eventually part ways with that particular team member.

We have learned that the best way to make your team members feel empowered is by allowing them to share their ideas on how to improve the business without judgment, chastisement, or reprimand. Will and I would always remind our team that there was no such thing as a bad idea in a brainstorming session. Will would take it as far as telling team members to give their craziest ideas—"the crazier, the better!" he would say.

Taking the time to listen to your team members' input and suggestions is important in building your team culture. This, however, requires humility by the founder and leadership team. A "know-it-all" leader will not only shun ideas or suggestions, but create an environment where team members will not approach them with ways in which the organization could potentially improve—a bad thing overall for the business.

Hire for attitude; train for skill.

This guiding principle is all about hiring people with the right attitude. In other words, we wanted to attract individuals who were loving, positive, and that radiated joy. Who really wants to work next to an angry ogre all day? I know that when I worked at the pharmacy I really disliked working with technicians who seemed to always be mopey and grumpy. It was a toxic environment, and I did not want that happening at our office! Therefore, we placed an emphasis on hiring people who were qualified for the job *and* had a great attitude. If their skillset was lackluster or needed fine-tuning to adapt them to our own systems and processes, we were willing to invest the time in doing so *only if they had a great personality.*

We had a few team members that presented well during their interviews with me that later turned out to be real ogres. Don't get me wrong, they were extraordinary performers and did top-notch work, but they had such a rotten attitude that no one in the office wanted to be near them. These individuals were quickly terminated. We also didn't want people with a great attitude but no skill set for the role we were hiring them for. This also didn't work because it would require too much investment in time to get them up to speed with their required tasks.

It was a careful balancing act of finding team members with *both* attitude and aptitude, with their attitude outweighing their technical skills. We provide a real life example of how we arrived at this principle when we share Ally's story in chapter 16.

Be accessible to the community.

This was basically a summary of our mission statement—*to provide exceptional dental care and to be a beacon of hope for our team members, patients, and community.* We wanted our services to be available to anyone in the community regardless of health status, insurance plan, etc. Everyone was welcome at American Pediatric Dental Group!

Provide a "wow experience" to all our guests.

We designed state-of-the-art, modern facilities that attracted not just children, but adolescents as well. We wanted parents and patients to be impressed by the decor and design of our office space. More importantly, however, we wanted our parents and patients to be blown away by the level of customer service that we offered. We wanted all our guests to say, "*Wow*, that was such a *great* experience!"

Therefore, we focused our training efforts on the human side of our business—properly greeting parents, demonstrating empathy, being patient and attentive, etc.—rather than focusing on simply "fixing teeth." In our opinion, the parents do not care if the dentistry rendered is stellar if the dentist and the team are rude or impatient with a child. What impressed parents the most was when the entire team, including the dentist, worked together to ensure that the dentistry was done in a loving, compassionate manner.

Nothing is impossible.

Will and I personally believe that nothing is impossible. "Impossible," in our opinion, is a self-imposed limitation by people who are unwilling to step outside their comfort zone. For example, I once thought that running a marathon (which I will cover in a future chapter) was "impossible." It turned out that it was not only possible, but I went on to complete two full marathons and over a dozen half-marathons in my running career. Similarly in business, we were told that our business model would never work, that it was "impossible." We silenced the negative chatter and dismissed the haters, and we not only proved that our model was possible, but it also served as a blueprint for many new offices that have recently opened in our community (more on that later).

We took this concept and applied it to everything we did. If we needed a task done a certain way or we needed to implement an automated solution that was not yet available, we would find a creative way to make it happen.

As an example, in many offices, patients are seen and later billed for services not covered by their insurance. Trying to collect money after services are rendered is difficult and results in the office's collection rate dropping. I didn't want this happening at our office, so we designed our insurance verification process to occur *before* the patient came to the office. Many offices didn't do it this way because it was a laborious process. Moreover, if the patient did not show up for their appointment, then the time invested verifying their insurance was wasted. I asked our insurance director her thoughts on verifying insurance and collecting payment *before services are rendered.* She gave me the usual slew of excuses: "It's too much work," "What if the patient doesn't show up for their appointment and we do all this work for nothing?" "No other office does it this way," etc. I calmly explained the rationale for my request and later asked her to do it in the manner I was proposing. She implemented this process begrudgingly, and we made a few tweaks along the way. Eventually, though, it proved to be a game changer, and our collection rate was an eye-dropping 99.8 percent.

Have serious fun—smile always!

A pediatric dental office can be a stressful environment. Parents and patients are nervous, the treatment is oftentimes difficult (imagine doing a filling or extraction on a three-year-old!), and the parental expectations of the dentist are extremely high (they want all the work to be done without the child crying). Imagine if the staff is also stressed and grumpy. This is a surefire recipe to team members losing their composure and taking out their frustrations on the patient—not a good scenario. In alignment with our principle of hiring team members with a positive and cheery attitude, we want our staff to be composed of individuals who are fun and loving, and we encourage them to listen to music (kid-appropriate, of course), interact with each other and with our parents, and create a fun atmosphere.

We celebrate mistakes—learn and grow.

Feedback from our patients—whether negative or positive—is very important in a service-oriented business. If we, as a business, did something wrong or we didn't meet our patient's expectations, we wanted to hear about it. The best lessons are the ones you learn from making a mistake. Similarly, when a team member made a mistake, we did not immediately reprimand him or her. Will and I believe that you either win *or you learn*, and we applied this principle with our team members. Did they do something positive? Great, let's celebrate it!

Did they make a mistake? Well, let's review and discuss it to get to the root of the problem. We would employ the Socratic Method by asking the person who made the mistake open-ended questions such as: "Why do you think this happened?" "In your opinion, how does this mistake impact the patient or the company?" "How can you rectify the situation?" "What can you do in the future to avoid making the same mistake?"

I clearly remember a situation that arose with a new front desk coordinator in our company's early days.

"I think I made a huge mistake, Richelle," the new front desk person nervously said.

Remaining calm, I asked, "Please walk me through what happened."

"I haven't been scheduling patients for their six-month dental appointment like we were supposed to," she said in a low tone, clearly distraught by what she had revealed to me.

In our business, not scheduling patients for their six-month dental appointment is an egregious error, one that could possibly lead to having no future patients on our schedule and loss of revenue. Taking this as a learning opportunity, I decided to have an ad hoc meeting with the entire front desk team to review the scheduling process. I figured that if one of my front desk coordinators had questions on how to properly schedule recall appointments, perhaps there were others on the team with the same inquiry.

I told the entire front desk team, "As you know, making an appointment for the parent six months in advance is important in making sure the child is up to date on their dental cleanings. In order for our computer system to send the parent automatic email and text reminders about the child's future dental cleaning appointment, they need to be on the schedule."

Then I proceeded to review the recall scheduling process, in detail, and answered any questions. When I found out that several front desk team members had questions or were unsure on how to properly schedule patients, I was happy I had taken the time to retrain them on this vital process.

I later approached the front desk coordinator who had admitted to the mistake initially and asked her if she was now clear on the process. She sighed in relief, said that she now understood it, and thanked me for taking the time to review the process rather than belittling her in front of her co-workers.

If I had yelled or simply reprimanded her for making a mistake, chances are high that she may have become disgruntled—or, worse, never tell me about a mistake again. Furthermore, I would have missed a golden opportunity to teach or review the scheduling process with the other front desk coordinators.

We offer autonomy, but expect accountability.

Will and I believe in empowering others as much as possible. We do this with our kids (we assign them roles in our home such as washing dishes, taking out the trash, etc.) and also at our business. We often refer to this principle as *delegate and elevate,* and it refers to assigning important tasks to people, trusting that these tasks will be completed, and if a mistake or mishap occurs, then the person doing the task would be accountable for amending their mistake.

The team member being assigned the role "owned" it and they had the independence—or autonomy—to carry out this role as best as they possibly could within our prescribed guidelines and protocols.

The team member was also expected to be responsible for mistakes if one was made (accountability).

Now, we would not just hand off an important process—for example, payroll processing or accounts payable—to anyone. We ensured that we hired the right person to do that particular job. In the aforementioned example, we made sure to hire the best HR specialist and accounting professional. After undergoing training, we laid out our expectations. For example, payroll needs to be processed biweekly, no later than 4:00 p.m. on the Thursday prior to payday.

We had a particular incident where the HR director forgot to submit the dentists' payroll on a Thursday. On Friday morning, we had sixteen angry dentists calling us asking why they had not gotten paid. I called the HR director, who was shocked at his memory lapse. He immediately liaised with our finance director, got paper checks, and delivered them personally to the dentists working at our offices.

Will was flustered with the director's error, but screaming at the HR director at that moment would not have been a good move (the HR director was busy resolving the issue, and taking time to discuss the issue with him would have delayed the dentists getting paid). Instead, Will waited until the issue was resolved, called the director, got his version of the facts (he came clean and admitted that he had forgotten to process payroll), and then later praised him for taking decisive action and quickly resolving the issue. Will understood that mistakes happen, but what really mattered for us was that the HR director was accountable for his actions and took the initiative to resolve the issue.

Get comfortable being uncomfortable—life begins outside your comfort zone.

This guiding principle is very dear to us, since we have followed this principle for as long as I can remember. Will and I have always swam against the current and done things differently from most people. We are not bound by the things we know or what is familiar (our comfort zone). Instead, we challenge the status quo and always ask ourselves, *What if?*

As a personal example, I had my kids pretty much back to back. I was pregnant with our children from 2010 until 2014, when we welcomed our last child. The only year within that time frame when I was not pregnant was in 2013. When our last child, Annabelle, was born in 2014, we yearned to travel, since we are wanderlusts and hadn't been able to travel as much while I was pregnant. Will surprised me during Christmas of that year with tickets to go to Hawaii, which is close to a twelve-hour trek from Florida. I was unsure if traveling with three kids under the age of three was a wise move. I asked him, "You think we can handle our kids on such a long plane ride? What if they start crying, or worse yet, they all start screaming?"

He wisely responded, "*What if* they *do* behave? I believe our kids will rise to our expectations of them. If you think they'll cry and misbehave, then they will. However, if we have high expectations for their behavior during our trip, they will likely meet those expectations." We always wanted our children to get accustomed to our jet-setting lifestyle and we didn't want to give it up for fear that our kids would misbehave and embarrass us. We were fearful, but we stepped outside our comfort zone and took the trip.

We showed up to the airport in Ft. Lauderdale with a baby, two toddlers, and an arsenal of bags, strollers, baby carriers, etc. People were shocked when they saw us walking through the airport with all our gear. They approached and asked us, "Where are you folks headed?"

We nonchalantly replied, "Oh, just Hawaii."

Their eyes widened so big that it looked as though they had seen a ghost! "Hawaii?! Well, that's over ten hours away! How are you gonna handle that plane ride with your kids?"

We confidently replied, "Don't worry, they'll behave."

Our kids ended up behaving exceedingly well on that trip. They truly blew away our expectations. We had manifested our expectations, and our kids delivered. When we got to Hawaii, people on our flight came up to congratulate us. We were proud parents, to say the least. That trip empowered us not just to visit even more far-flung destinations with our children (we have been to over thirty countries with our children as of the writing of this book), but also to attend festivals, concerts, and fine-dining establishments with them (we even had high tea at the Ritz hotel when we visited London a few years ago).

Because we stepped outside our comfort zone, we saw what was possible. We encourage our team at work to do the same by learning new skills, taking on more responsibility, and making critical decisions on their own.

Our trip to Hawaii with three kids under the age of 3 years old.

Take initiative—if there's a problem, offer a solution.

Will and I believed that our team should be proactive and find solutions to problems that inevitably arise. We didn't just want them to throw up their hands and freeze when faced with a problem. Instead, we wanted them to think about possible solutions and propose them to us or their managers. This created an efficient work environment where workflows were not hampered by team members not knowing how to proceed when issues arose. The goal was to find solutions to problems as quickly as possible.

Team members often came up to me and said, "Richelle, I have a problem." Before they could explain the nature of their issue, I would immediately ask them, "If you have a problem, have you figured out a way to solve it?" If they had not, I would ask them to return when they had a possible solution. For us, it didn't matter if the solution was good or not. What was important was the fact that the individual at least took initiative and thought of a way to resolve the issue.

Trust, but verify.

This principle ties in with one of the previous: *We offer autonomy, but expect accountability.* Will and I often delegated tasks to our team, but we had checks and balances to verify that the task was being completed correctly.

As an example, at our offices, the office manager submits the insurance claims of all the patients seen throughout the day. These claims are then processed by the insurance company, which then sub-mits payment to us. Since this is such an important process, we *trust* that the office manager submits these claims daily, but we also have an independent insurance specialist *verify* that all claims for all the offices are accurate prior to submitting them. We have had incidents where the office manager forgot to submit the claims at the end of the day, causing us to miss insurance payments for services rendered. The system of checks and balances by the insurance specialist ensured a safeguard against incidents like that happening again in the future.

Always, always do what is right for the patient!

This last principle is one of the most important principles of our *Credo.* It serves as a guiding light in every decision we make and every action we take. When we prioritized the well-being and best interests of the patient above all else, we ensured that we were providing the highest quality of care possible. Doing what was right for the patient meant going beyond simply treating a patient's cavities, infection, or pain. It meant taking the time to understand their unique needs, concerns, and preferences.

This principle also demanded that we maintain the utmost integrity in our interactions with parents and caregivers. We were always transparent and honest, providing them with accurate information about their child's dental condition, treatment options, and potential risks and benefits. By doing so, we empowered them to make informed choices about their child's healthcare.

For instance, it was not uncommon for us to come across children who had significant dental issues and suffered from dental phobias as a result of previous traumatic encounters. Consequently, these patients were uncooperative during the dental appointments to fix their teeth. Other times we may have had a child that lacked the mental maturity to get the dental treatment done. In these cases, we informed the parent why the recommended dental treatment was needed and offered treatment options—sedation, for example—that would facilitate the treatment without further harming the child's psyche. For us, it was about the *experience* of both child and parents, and not simply rendering treatment that may have the potential of permanently traumatizing a child.

Now that we have reviewed our guiding principles in detail and described how we used these to shape our organizational culture, I will now let Will describe the opening day of our business—a day that was both exciting, but nerve-racking for both of us. Although Will and I had put in countless hours of hard work and preparation, there was still a sense of uncertainty about what lay ahead. We had done our best to drum up interest and create buzz in the community, but we were both unsure of how patients would respond to our business. It's one thing to have a dream and a well thought out plan, but it's an entirely different experience when the business actually opens and your theories are put to the test.

Chapter Eleven

Game Over?

William Peña

OUR OFFICE FINALLY OPENED on November 11, 2011. It took us nearly a year and a half from the day we closed on the loans until final completion of our office construction. It was a grueling process getting all the loan documents prepared and submitted to the bank that was financing our project. Although we were overwhelmed with the amount of due diligence the bank required, we were happy that we had taken the first step toward opening our own business. Fortunately, Richelle was by my side during the initial stages of our office planning. She empathized with my frustration as she was simultaneously busy developing marketing advertisements for our business and experiencing her own sense of overwhelm.

Since both of us needed to be at the new office early, we hired a nanny to take care of Adrian. Having to leave our baby so early in the morning and not being able to see him until later in the evening was probably one of the hardest challenges of being first-time parents and new business owners. It felt like we were dividing our precious and limited time between two things that we were truly passionate about excelling in. However, we found some consolation in the fact that our business required our attention. While we longed to stay at home and be with Adrian, we understood the importance of dedicating the necessary time to ensure the survival of our business.

It is worth mentioning that our initial office was established during the tail end of the Great Recession—a period marked by massive unemployment and an economic downturn as a result of the housing crisis that ensued from the slipshod mortgage underwriting practices of banks and poor oversight by regulators. Despite the uncertain economic climate and the presence of numerous pediatric dentists in the city where we opened our office, we maintained a positive outlook.

Richelle and I were extremely excited and hopeful for our new venture. We had established a company with a strong purpose, had hired team members that "fit in" with our servant-leadership culture, and we were ready to save the world. The only problem was we had no patients on the schedule, our phones were not ringing with patients wanting an appointment, and we had to quickly decipher what to do before the working capital the bank had given us would run out.

The other issue we faced was our insurance payor model, in which the payment is processed by the patient's insurance company and may take over a month from the patient's appointment for us to receive it. So, if we saw a patient today, as an example, we would not get paid by their insurance carrier until approximately four to six weeks later.

In the meantime, we had expenses, such as rent, employee salaries, supplies, etc., that needed to be paid, and as a result, our cash reserves began to quickly dwindle.

Initially, our patient schedule relied heavily on the support of our family and friends. It was heartwarming to have our niece, Leilani, and nephew, Isaiah, as two of our first patients. However, during periods when our schedule had gaps and we didn't have patients, Richelle and I took matters into our own hands. We embarked on what we called "doctor runs," where we visited local pediatrician offices, general dentists, and orthodontists in our community. Our goal was to distribute our marketing materials and introduce our new office to these healthcare professionals. Additionally, we extended our outreach to elementary schools, children's entertainment venues, and local daycares. We conducted show-and-tell presentations, sharing information about our services and handing out marketing materials. Our approach was simple—we wanted to reach out to any local business that catered to children and families. We believed that having a beautiful, state-of-the-art office was meaningless if no one knew about us. Our aim was to spread the word in the community, highlighting our competitive advantages such as the insurances we accepted and the specialized services we offered.

Our efforts slowly began paying off. Patients began trickling in, and they absolutely loved the experience, but it was still not enough to stymie the cash bleed of our business. By this point, we were almost eight weeks into operating our office, and although we had some patients on the schedule, we still needed to see many more to prevent our business from failing.

Needless to say, Richelle and I were extremely stressed. I began experiencing self-doubt, asking myself, *Did I make the right move opening an office in a saturated area? Will our business model really work, or is it just a pipe dream? Will we survive as a company, or will I have to go back to work with another pediatric dentist and face the embarrassment of having failed? What are Richelle and our family going to think of me? What will my children think of me when they grow up?*

I pondered on these questions constantly. Also, I suffered from insomnia and I began experiencing acute bouts of anxiety where I could hardly breathe thinking about the dire situation of our business.

To make matters worse, I would see my son sleeping peacefully in his crib and wonder why I had not simply followed the traditional path of working for someone else while building my new office. *Was I that confident—or deranged—to think that my business model would actually work and that patients would come flocking in? Was I delusional?* I was a thirty-one-year-old healthcare professional, living at his in-laws' house with his wife and son, whose business was faltering. To say that the pressure I felt was high is an understatement.

I was extremely grateful, however, to have Richelle by my side during these difficult times. She not only supported me, but she also reaffirmed her commitment to the success of our business. She would tell me, "Will, it takes time to build a business. Trust me, anything that is worthwhile is difficult in the beginning. Don't worry, babe, it will get better. I'm with you to the end."

Her words had such a huge impact on me. Although I had self-doubt and was down on myself, her words encouraged me to persevere. Honestly, I am not sure if I would have had the wherewithal to continue if I didn't have Richelle by my side. Her positivity and tenacity gave me strength. Without her, I most likely would have failed.

In hindsight, I would say that I placed too much pressure on myself. I was so eager to prove my business theories right that I was scared, flustered, and anxious when patients did not come rushing in on our first day of business. I had not yet understood the power of patience and perseverance. All I knew at that point was that we were several weeks into our business, our money was quickly running out, and the demand that I was eagerly expecting had not yet materialized. It was an important business (and life) lesson, no doubt. However, when you are seeing your business failing and you feel that all eyes are on you, you may easily crack under the pressure.

Chapter Twelve

The Power of Persistence

Richelle Peña

I KNEW WE WERE in trouble when our office had been open for several weeks and we did not make nearly enough money to cover our expenses. We were heavily relying on the working capital provided by the bank, and it was draining fast! I had personally marketed the office, helped make important connections with other healthcare individuals in the community, and did everything in my power to properly train the team on providing customer service. But, it was not enough. We had to do more and faster.

We made the decision to withdraw our personal savings account and invest that money into our business. It was our "all-or-nothing" moment. Although this cash infusion helped support the business, we needed to find a way to attract more patients to the practice and get their insurance carriers to begin paying us. As Will mentioned, patients' insurance plans would take over a month to pay for the services we did, so although we were seeing patients at the office, we were delayed in receiving payments.

One day, I noticed Will distraught, quietly driving on our commute home. He looked at me—with a weary look on his face—and told me, "Love, we have less than a month's worth of money in our business account. If we don't see more patients and generate more money, I am not sure if our company will survive."

My mind quickly goes into overdrive when faced with a calamity. I am not one to wallow in self-pity or get down on myself. I simply start thinking of what I can do to resolve the situation.

I quickly replied, "Will, I have an idea. Why don't I sell my wedding ring? It's probably worth several thousand dollars. We could use that money to pay for our payroll next week."

Will turned to me with watery eyes. With a slight tremble in his voice, he said, "I don't know what to say. That is such a generous gesture and I am eternally grateful for your unwavering support. I feel horrible for dragging you into this situation. I promised you that our business would be a success, and here we are debating whether to sell the wedding ring that my mom helped me buy for you. I'll keep it in mind, but I want to explore other options before we ultimately decide to sell it. That is definitely the option of last resort."

I replied, "You did not drag me into anything. I believe in this company, and most importantly, I believe in *you*. I know that God put a promise in our hearts to create a company that would help those less fortunate, and He will help us see it through. He wouldn't have brought us this far to let us fail. He has a plan for us, and we need to have faith in Him. Don't worry, everything will be okay. I have a strong feeling."

When I say, "I have a strong feeling," it is because I know that however dire a situation may seem, God will help us resolve it. It is my faith that has helped me in my most difficult moments, and during that grim period of late 2011—when it seemed as though our dream was crumbling before us—I tried my best to instill that same hope and optimism in Will.

Don't get me wrong. Will is a man of faith, but sometimes when the weight of the world is on your shoulders (as it was for Will as the leader of the company), it is oftentimes difficult to see the big picture. You may lose the forest for the trees. To remedy this, I was always by his side to point out the bigger picture, to let him know that our business stood for a noble purpose and that God would not let us fail.

It is for this reason that having a clearly defined purpose or "why" is crucial when starting a business. It serves as a guiding force during challenging times and helps you stay focused on the bigger picture. There will inevitably be moments of adversity and doubt, but having a strong purpose for your business, along with faith in a higher power, can provide clarity and perspective.

Over the next week or so, the business continued to falter. We simply could not produce enough to offset our expenses. Will, again, had a crucial conversation with me, this time at the office after work.

He told me, "Richelle, the situation is bad. We have run through most of our cash. Do you think it's possible for you to return to work at least part-time so that you can generate some income?" I was hesitant, but I'm a team player, and I'll put my apprehension aside when it comes time to fend for our business or family.

Although we were building our business together, I could not fully grasp the pressure that Will was under. He had taken a leap of faith and had quit his job to dedicate himself fully to building his office, had asked me to quit my job and join him on this venture, and now the business was not trending as he had expected it. I can only imagine the sense of culpability that he must have felt during those moments. I did my best to understand his personal situation, and I did whatever was needed to drive the business forward.

I, too, was feeling overwhelmed because I had a newborn at home and was experiencing "mommy guilt." Adrian was born with jaundice and needed frequent checkups with his pediatrician to check his bilirubin levels. I did my best to balance my responsibilities at work with taking care of my son, and I would take him to his pediatrician appointments as much as I could. My parents also helped take him to see his physician during those times when my work schedule made it impossible. I was devastated about not being fully committed to Adrian's health as a newborn, but our business was our livelihood and at that point, it desperately needed our attention.

I told Will, "Yes, let me call my manager at Target and ask if they still have a vacancy." I called my former supervisor, and he gracefully allowed me to work at the pharmacy again.

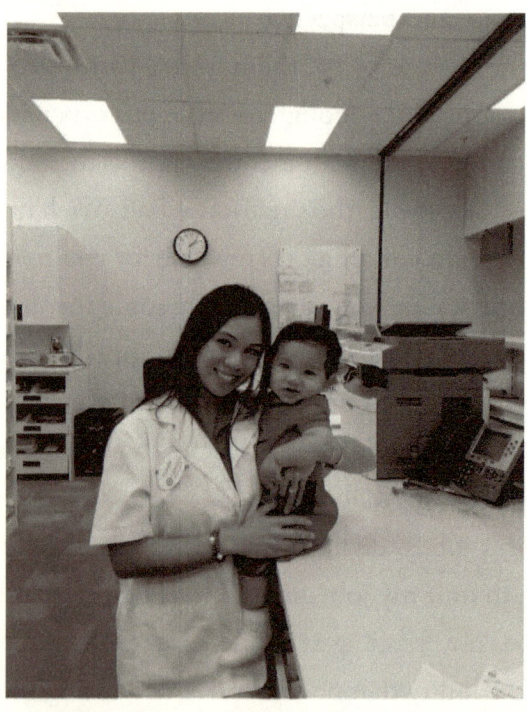

Working at the pharmacy to help sustain our business. I really looked forward to seeing my 7-month old son, Adrian, pass by and visit me.

While I was actively working on generating buzz and increasing visibility for our business, I stumbled upon the contact details of the events coordinator at the local city council, a woman by the name of Mary. During our conversation, Mary expressed an interest in collaborating with a dentist from our community. This partnership would grant us valuable access to various community events and promotional opportunities at local schools. Without hesitation, I eagerly registered for this promising partnership.

Little did I know how impactful this connection with Mary was going to be for our business and how meeting her was going to change our course.

Mary told me that the city council was hosting a holiday party, and she insisted that we rent a booth to promote our services since that event had had a great turnout in the past. We readily agreed.

Will and I, along with our staff, attended at the event and promoted our office. We networked with the other vendors present at the event, hosted games in our booth, and spoke passionately about the services we offered to the individuals in attendance. Will even dressed up in a tooth costume and danced merrily by our booth to attract families. It worked! We collected over a hundred potential leads for our business from that single event.

That event, along with the increasing number of referrals from pediatrician offices, really began filling our patient schedule. Will was now working in the clinic full-time seeing patients. Patients began writing positive reviews about our business and were relaying back to their pediatricians what a memorable experience they had at our office. We knew this, of course, because Adrian's pediatrician was one of our top referrals in the community! When I came to the office with Adrian for his checkups, he would praise Will and me for the incredible work that we were doing and urged us to continue our mission. It was great to see that our efforts were finally paying off!

At one point, we became so busy that Will, with evident chagrin, told me, "Richelle, I don't know how to tell you this since you just started your job at the pharmacy, but I need you to come back to work at the office. Whatever you did, I need you to continue doing it. We are bursting at the seams, and I need your help!"

Not only did we have patients on the schedule, Will explained, but the patients' insurance carriers had started paying us from the previous months, and from that point on we were getting paid on a weekly basis.

We were filled with gratitude as we witnessed God's response to our prayers. We realized the significance of His assistance and guidance in all that we had achieved thus far. The unwavering belief that anything is achievable with God by our side became our guiding light as Will and I continued our difficult journey of entrepreneurship.

Upon hearing Will's news, my mouth dropped open. So many thoughts went through my head. *What am I going to tell my manager at Target? Do I quit again, after only one month? What is my boss going to think?*

I was nervous about having the dreaded conversation with my boss, who just a few weeks prior had welcomed me back to my former job. But, nevertheless, I mustered the courage to talk with him, I explained the situation, and I gave him my two weeks' notice. My boss was flabbergasted. He had taken a leap of faith by rehiring me, and here I was putting in my resignation a few weeks into the job. He told me with noticeable frustration in his voice, "Richelle, I gave you an opportunity, and after only five weeks, you are quitting on me to rejoin your husband's company. I have nothing further to say to you. Good luck to you and your husband on your new venture."

I knew that I had closed a door, but it was a risk I was willing to take. I knew that if, God forbid, our dental business once again floundered, I could not call my pharmacy supervisor and readily ask him for another job opportunity. I understood this, but I intuitively knew that I would not need to return to the pharmacy. I was reinvigorated by my accomplishments in the dental business and knew that I could build on my prior successes. I had been able to create strategic alliances with key people in the community, and I knew that I could continue leveraging my relationships to help our business succeed.

When I got back to our company, I continued my marketing efforts and began liaising with Mary and other community leaders. I focused my efforts on participating in direct community outreach events and invested heavily in having a presence in the majority of these events taking place throughout the city.

Since most of these events were in the evenings or on weekends, Will and I would work at the office seeing patients and we would later set up our booth at the park or other venue where the event was taking place. I would ask my parents to bring Adrian so that at least we could spend time with him while Will and I promoted our office. Afterward, we would catch a late-night dinner as a family.

Looking back, I am amazed that we had the energy to endure those hard moments of building our business and raising a family. Those moments are honestly like a blur to me now. We were juggling so many things at once that seconds, hours, and days all coalesced into one.

I was proud of myself. Because of my hard work and tenacity, I had managed to spread awareness of our pediatric dental services and drive patients to our new office. We had new patients on the schedule for several weeks, and our phones were ringing nonstop with patients requesting an appointment. It was a painfully slow start in the first few months after we opened, but once word got out about our office, we could simply not keep up with the demand. Will and I both breathed a sigh of relief, realizing that God had pulled us from the brink of financial ruin. We had survived as a company, at least for the time being.

It is important to mention that in the early stages of launching our business, we were fully committed to its success. However, we also recognized the importance of striking a balance between growing our business and maintaining healthy personal relationships. Despite our hectic schedules, we both eagerly made time to spend with our son, Adrian. We took turns bathing and feeding him in the evenings when we got home from work, with Will insisting on putting him to sleep. After I breastfed Adrian, Will would lovingly rock him until he drifted off to sleep.

On certain days, I would even carve out an hour or two to spend time with my son. I enrolled Adrian in a music class to create meaningful moments with him. For Will and me, the focus was not on the quantity of time spent with our children, but rather on the *quality* of that time. The two weekly one-hour music classes were a refreshing break and brought me immense joy. Occasionally, Will would also join us for the classes.

Our busy work schedules and the demands of raising our son, however, had taken a toll on our marriage. The constant stress and lack of sleep had left us feeling exhausted and disconnected. We noticed that we were becoming short-tempered with each other and arguing over trivial matters. It became clear that our lack of quality time together was the root cause of our constant bickering. While we worked side by side at the office and commuted together, we did not consider that to be quality time. Our conversations revolved around work and our son's routine, leaving little room for meaningful connection.

Recognizing the importance of nurturing our marriage amidst our busy schedules, we came up with a plan to prioritize weekly date nights. Those occasions didn't require extravagant outings or elaborate plans, as time was a precious commodity for us. Instead, we opted for simple yet meaningful activities like going out for dinner and a movie. On occasions when time was limited, we would create a cozy atmosphere at home by purchasing a bottle of wine and some cheese, indulging in a delightful charcuterie board. Other times, we would unwind with a glass of pinot noir while enjoying a movie or a captivating Netflix series. The key was to carve out dedicated time for us as a couple, especially during challenging periods at work and home.

Chapter Thirteen

Big Hairy Audacious Goals

William Peña

TILL THIS DAY, I am extremely grateful for Richelle's magnanimous gesture to part ways with her wedding ring in order to save the business. Words fail to describe the deep appreciation and love I feel for my wife, who is the most selfless and loyal person I know. Not many people are willing to sacrifice so much because they believe in someone else's dream. I owed it to Richelle and my kids to honor my commitments and provide them with the life I had promised.

I am also thankful that we didn't have to resort to such drastic measures. I would've never forgiven myself for selling such a significant item that is a symbol of our holy matrimony. To be completely honest, I don't think I would've had the courage to move forward with such a decision. If, God forbid, it had come to that, I would have simply allowed the business to fail.

Fortunately, God intervened just before hitting rock bottom and we hit a strong inflection point that propelled our company toward success. It reminded me of the well-known saying, "When you hit rock bottom, you have nowhere to go but up."

Once we were past the "death stage" of our business (and once we were able to breathe a sigh of relief), we focused on growing. In January of 2012, three months after we opened our office, we planned a community open house and invited local healthcare professionals, the mayor, and family to attend. It was a great turnout! We took pictures with all our guests and were so happy that we were finally doing well.

At one point throughout the event, an invitee asked me, "Dr. Peña, why is the name of your practice American Pediatric Dental *Group*? Do you have other doctors working here, or perhaps business partners?" With a wicked smile, I replied, "No, Richelle and I are the entire group. There are no other dentists working here but me, and my only business partner is my wife, Richelle."

She had the nerve to actually snicker at my comment, saying, "That's not a *group*; that's only you!" and then she abruptly turned around and briskly walked away.

Although I was initially shocked by her audacity, I was unmoved by her cynicism and her facetious comment. Richelle and I have always believed that you need to set a big vision for what you eventually want to become and not just focus on short-term goals.

After the open house, Richelle and I were sitting on the sofa gleefully speaking about the event that we had just hosted while looking at the photographs we had taken. Richelle was wearing a fitted, long skirt, and I noticed a slight bulge in her abdominal area in a picture we took with our son, Adrian. She noticed the bulge as well and asked me, "Will, do you think I look fat in this picture?" This was clearly a very loaded question, and I had to find the most politically correct answer to give her.

Nervously, I said, "You know, I have noticed a slight distension of your belly over the last couple of days, but it's probably nothing.

It's probably because you are getting your period." She then told me, "Babe, I haven't gotten my period this month. I'm late!"

I was quiet for a few seconds as I processed what she had just told me. I quickly turned to her and said, "Babe, you think you may be pregnant?"

She quickly replied, "Will, go to the pharmacy and buy a pregnancy test, right now!"

I immediately drove to the pharmacy and bought the test. When I came back, Richelle took it, and lo and behold, she was pregnant! When she saw the positive result on the test stick, she panicked.

She told me, "Oh my God, Will, we have a six-month-old child, and I'm pregnant again! What are we going to do? We are living at my parents' house, and we just went through three brutal months trying to keep the business afloat, and now here I am pregnant with another child!"

During the course of her panic attack, she turned to me and noticed a huge smile on my face. I simply started laughing and told her, "This is a miracle! I'm so happy! We are going to have another baby. You should be happy, too. God wouldn't have given us another baby if we couldn't handle it. We are going to be okay. Stop worrying!"

The open house of our first dental office. This is the picture we were viewing when Richelle noticed a slight distension in her belly. Adrian was 6-months old and Richelle was approximately 1-month pregnant with Leia.

I was honestly overwhelmed with joy knowing that our family was growing. Were there many unknowns? Absolutely! But I knew that a child was a miracle from God, and I chose not to worry. Besides, I love kids and I was ecstatic to see our family growing.

We both knew that continuing to build our business while parenting two young children was going to be challenging. Yes, we had a strong support system. We had our parents and family to step in and help us. But, Richelle and I had always wanted to raise and nurture our own family, to have kids so that we could spend quality time with them. Being present in their lives was a priority for both of us, but we also had to deal with the demands of a business that was catching momentum and was at the cusp of growing exponentially.

It was a dilemma, and it felt as though we had to choose between growing our business or growing our family. Guilt and self-doubt once again began creeping in. *Were we doing the right thing by continuing to grow our business? Could we just be happy with simply owning a single practice? Was the delayed gratification of postponing buying our dream home and making money now versus reinvesting it back into growing the business worth it?*

Richelle and I had a shared vision—we wanted to own a *business* and not simply work at a *job*. The distinction between the two being that a business can function without the owner/founder having to directly intervene in its operations, whereas if the business cannot survive without the owner present, then this becomes a *job*. We knew that we needed to create a business—with its requisite systems and processes, strong team, and auditing checklists—to achieve time and financial freedom so that we could, in due time, spend more quality time with our family and pursue our own personal goals. As Arnold Scharzenegger states in his book, *Be Useful. Seven Tools for Life*, "To have a clear vision is to have a picture of what you want your life to look like and a plan for how to get there."

Even though Richelle and I shared the desire to create a business that would provide us with time and financial freedom, we had different visions regarding the scale of our company. I envisioned our business expanding nationwide with dental offices in every state. On the other hand, Richelle's goal was to establish a strong presence solely in the south Florida region. Despite this disparity in our entrepreneurial goals, we decided to adopt a "wait-and-see" approach and allow the business itself to dictate its growth trajectory. We understood that the demands and opportunities that arose would guide us in determining the extent of our expansion.

In hindsight, my ambition stemmed from a strong desire to be a leader of a major corporation. Ever since I was a child, I looked up to business leaders. I admired, for example, how my parents bootstrapped their way to creating a multimillion-dollar manufacturing business through their hard work and perseverance. Later on in college, I began voraciously reading business and leadership books, and I was enamored by the respect that business leaders commanded through their accomplishments. I wanted this for me, too. I wanted respect and admiration, and I believed that the only way to accomplish this was by creating a major company with a national presence. I had no idea how "unbalanced" these leaders were and the sacrifices that they had to make to reach their success. I was naive in thinking that I could be a leader of a major corporation and still be fully present with my family. I had not yet learned that everything in life has a price. The price I needed to pay—time away from my family to pursue my entrepreneurial dreams—was too high of a price, and I was unwilling to do this. I would find this out the hard way along my journey.

In the meantime, however, we continued working hard building our business. By the time we had our open house, we were profitable, and we had a strong demand for our services (as evidenced by our full schedule that spanned several weeks). By the end of our first year in business, we hired another pediatric dentist to work with us full time.

Things were definitely looking rosy, especially with the arrival of our baby girl, Leia.

Chapter Fourteen

The G.F.B. Principle

William Peña

AFTER NEARLY A YEAR in business, our eldest daughter, Leia, was born on August 31, 2012. We named her "Leia," because it means "child of heaven" in Hawaiian culture. The name resonated with us because we felt that despite what we were confronting at work and the challenges that awaited us with having two babies at home, she was a miracle from God. When Leia was born, I officially became a "girl dad." I had always wanted to have a boy and a girl because both genders seemed so different to me. Holding my little girl in my hands was surreal. It was love at first sight. I kissed her tiny forehead and whispered a little prayer in her ear. As I had told Adrian, I promised to be a great father to my little princess.

My son, Adrian, and Leia are only fourteen months apart, so having a toddler and newborn at home was a bit challenging. Luckily, we were still living with my in-laws, so they were able to help us out. I had heard the saying, "It takes a village to raise a family," but it was not until my daughter was born that I truly understood and valued this common wisdom.

Richelle and I are grateful and appreciative for her parents' help and support with our two young kids. We had been in business for close to a year by this point and we were busy having meetings with our team, participating in community events as part of our grassroots efforts to market our services directly to the community, and I was seeing a full schedule of patients in the clinic. Without their help, it would have been really difficult for us to grow a business and raise a young family at the same time.

Then, when Leia was eleven months old, I unexpectedly lost my mother. She had battled health ailments her entire life, and a sudden-onset epileptic seizure claimed her life. Losing a loved one so suddenly and at such a young age (my mom was only fifty-two years old when she passed away) shakes you to the core and really makes you focus on what is truly important in life.

In the aftermath of my mom's death, I began a long period of introspection. I began by taking a spiritual inventory of how I had lived my life up to that point. This was when I decided to rearrange my life's priorities in order of importance.

I began asking myself, *Is this really how I wanted to live my life, constantly stressed and anxious about the business? Would any of what I was doing really matter in the long run if my health was affected? Would I hamper my family's joy and happiness with my constant worrying?*

Although the business was doing well financially at the time and we were fortunate to be growing our organization, we faced an increasing number of managerial issues. For one, dealing with Medicaid involves a lot of paperwork and a careful amount of compliance checks that we quickly had to learn. Moreover, since we were seeing an increased number of patients, we needed to quickly hire staff members to keep up with our demand. Richelle and I needed to recruit people that were a true fit with our business culture and this is not always easy to do, especially when you need to fill vacancies in a timely manner. Fortunately, we could use the situational-based question approach that Richelle had brought over from Target to recruit rock-stars to our team, but recruitment is still a pain-stakingly long and arduous process. Lastly, we had internal operational issues that needed to be handled. We needed to learn how to effectively schedule patients, handle equipment maintenance, manage our employee benefits, etc.

There was so much to do that it quickly became overwhelming. It was even more stressful having to learn all these things almost simultaneously, and still see a full schedule of patients in the clinic, perform sedations on select days, and also treat patients under general anesthesia at the local children's hospital. The pace was relentless. I would see patients in the clinic and during lulls in the schedule or after the clinic was over, I would quickly meet with Richelle to figure out a solution to a problem, or address a concern from an angry parent. When running a business, there never seems to be an end to issues or problems.

Richelle was becoming increasingly concerned over seeing me struggle with insomnia and the constant stress of managing the business. I reassured her, perhaps to reassure myself as well, that the stress I was feeling was only temporary and a normal part of being an entrepreneur. I explained that once the business became more self-sustaining, the stress would become more manageable. However, the pressure I was under led me to develop unhealthy eating habits as a way to cope, resulting in a weight gain of nearly twenty pounds within a year.

I made the conscious decision to actively engage in self-improvement. To begin with, I decided to drastically improve my diet, which was abysmal. At that time, my eating habits consisted mainly of consuming unhealthy processed foods, frequently dining out, and indulging in a plethora of red meat. Considering the numerous cardiac problems my mother experienced, I made the switch to a pescatarian diet and started incorporating more fruits and vegetables into my meals. To complement my dietary changes, I also made sure to stay hydrated by drinking plenty of water throughout the day.

In addition to improving my diet, I incorporated regular exercise into my routine. This combination of healthy eating and physical activity helped me shed excess weight, build muscle, and increase my endurance. I started with simple workouts like walking on a treadmill and gradually progressed to more intense activities like running, weightlifting, and cycling.

I also rearranged my life's priorities in order of importance and arrived at the *G.F.B. (God, Family, Business) Principle.*

My top priority is to dedicate myself to serving God and upholding His honor in every aspect of my life. I honor Him by being a good person, with a strong moral compass so I can be a positive role model for my kids and for the children I interact with on a daily basis. In my work as a pediatric dentist, I utilize my talents not for personal gain, but rather to relieve the pain and suffering of children afflicted with dental decay and infections. Moreover, I lean heavily on my faith and God's guidance to navigate through tough decisions and overcome challenges that arise in my life. Consequently, I place significant importance on nurturing a profound spiritual connection with Him.

Once I have fulfilled my pious obligations as a Catholic, I prioritize my family above all else. It is important to me to spend quality time with them, explore the world together, and fully engage with my children, being present for all of their activities and achievements. My utmost desire is for my kids to possess enduring memories of their father actively participating in their lives. I am cognizant of the fact that I only have a limited number of years with them before they mature, become adults, and establish their own families. Therefore,

I am determined to cherish the time we have while they still live at home with their mother and me.

I came to the conclusion that once I was able to satisfy the first two priorities, I would then focus on growing the business.

Laying out my life's priorities was eye-opening for me. I felt that I now had an actual plan that would help guide me through the multitude of decisions that I needed to make in my personal life and in business. By having a list of priorities that was important and resonated with me, I could focus intently on what I wanted to accomplish with my life.

Several months following the unfortunate loss of my mother, I had a heartfelt conversation with Richelle, where I opened up about my emotions and shared the concept of the G.F.B. principle. I explained to her that my life's focal point would now revolve around this principle. To my delight, she wholeheartedly embraced this renewed focus. She expressed relief and happiness upon learning that we now shared a common vision for both our company and our personal lives. It was gratifying to know that I was placing my well-being and our family above the demands of the business. From her perspective, it seemed that I was simply adopting her way of life, albeit with a slight delay in fully recognizing its value.

She also liked the idea of having our life's priority spelled out and delineated, so she adopted this *G.F.B. Principle* for herself and to this day, we are faithful disciples.

Chapter Fifteen

Paying Our Dues

Richelle Peña

WITH A RENEWED FOCUS on our life, we began shifting our priorities at work. Will and I were committed to improving the management of our current assets by establishing effective systems and processes, allowing us to have more quality time as a family. This priority was further emphasized when I gave birth to our daughter, Annabelle, on October 5, 2014.

When Annabelle was born, we had three children under the age of three! Although we already had Adrian and Leia and knew the routine, I was concerned that we were now outnumbered. Nevertheless, I held this little miracle in my arms, and despite being in discomfort from the cesarean section that I had just endured, I immediately felt a surge of love for my little princess. We named our daughter "Annabelle" as a homage to Will's mom, who had passed away the year before. "Ana" was his mom's first name, and "Belle" is French for "beautiful."

Craziness and pandemonium described our home situation at the time, but Will and I loved every single minute of it. We knew that the madness would not last forever and that our kids would one day grow up. Instead of longing for the toddler and infancy stage to pass quickly, we embraced it and fully immersed ourselves in the present moment. Our previous experience with Adrian and Leia gave us a sense of confidence in our parenting abilities. The sleepless nights, endless feedings, diaper changes, and the never-ending task of washing baby bottles no longer seemed daunting. Although we were outnumbered with three children now, we found joy and fulfillment in every precious moment.

As Will's mom used to remind us, "Children do not belong to the parents. They belong to the world. So, when they are with you, enjoy them. Enjoy every single moment of their company." Her wise words are deeply ingrained in our hearts, and we make it a point to spend quality time with our children no matter how many things we have going on or how busy we are.

In fact, every year Will and I blocked out approximately forty days of vacation that we used to travel the world—a tradition that we continue to do till this day. For us, this is an investment in our family time, a time we never take for granted.

I had written in a previous chapter about our trip to Hawaii and how this changed our outlook for traveling with our kids. Prior to that trip, we were apprehensive about traveling with children so young. It is worth reiterating, since I know many parents are fearful of traveling with their kids, that your children will act in accordance with your expectations of them.

Will and I genuinely believe that our children will behave properly when we go out to eat or when we travel; and they usually do, oftentimes exceeding our expectations. It's similar to what the book *The Secret* proposes—manifest your desires, and you will attract them into your life.

After the Hawaii trip, we continued traveling as a family of wanderlusts. We have visited places such as Iceland, Abu Dhabi, Marrakesh,

Austria, Bora Bora, Switzerland, and even the Philippines, with our three kids in tow.

Have we had hard moments on flights or had unforeseen things happen to us while visiting a foreign country? Of course! But we didn't allow those small moments to ruin the fun and enjoyment of traveling together.

After Annabelle was born, we decided that it was finally time to purchase our first home. It had been three years since we started the business, and thankfully it was doing well. We also needed the extra space for all of our kids' toys, playpens, cribs, etc. In September of 2014, we became homeowners. We were overwhelmed with gratitude that we were finally able to purchase a beautiful home in a great neighborhood. We had sacrificed a lot throughout the years, and had followed an unorthodox path by living with my parents despite being healthcare professionals.

The sacrifice, however, had paid off.

In 2015, we made the decision to expand our business by opening two additional offices. We saw growth opportunities in two distinct markets and we decided to open up both offices simultaneously. One of the key factors that contributed to our ability to expand was the team of talented individuals we had hired. We were fortunate to have team members who not only excelled in their respective roles but also showed great potential for leadership. Their dedication and competence allowed us to delegate tasks and responsibilities, relieving some of the burden on us as business owners.

While running a business will always come with its fair share of stress and unexpected challenges, we grew more adept at managing issues more effectively. For example, we learned how to deal with intransigent parents and their outlandish requests and expectations, and we learned to navigate through unexpected equipment failures or technical glitches. We were growing in our leadership roles within the company and it was satisfying to see the impact we were having on the company.

As the company grew, I continued in my role as marketing director, attracting new patients to all our offices, especially the new ones. In addition to my marketing role, I also took on the task of overseeing the operations of our offices. Since there was no designated person in charge of operations, I stepped in to ensure that our staff performed their tasks efficiently and effectively. This involved personally visiting our offices and verifying that our team members were handling phone calls professionally, submitting insurance claims accurately, and completing their end-of-day tasks as required.

Although my primary focus was on marketing, I recognized the importance of supporting the smooth functioning of our offices. By taking on these additional responsibilities, I aimed to contribute to the overall success of our business and ensure that our patients received the highest level of care and service.

While it was challenging to juggle both marketing and operations, I did my best to manage the offices and support Will in his role as the primary dental care provider.

At this stage, Will and I found ourselves engaged in constant arguments regarding the performance of our offices. Just like with our first office, Will expressed concerns about the slow growth in patient numbers, the depletion of our working capital, and the recurring financial losses. Although we had the experience of building our first practice, we had tripled in size in a relatively short amount of time. The amount of work that needed to be done to manage our company and its operations increased significantly as well.

Although we were both stressed from the pressures of work, we made it a rule to never talk about work when we were home. We had a few heated work-related conversations prior to formulating this rule, so we decided, unanimously, to refrain from talking about issues that had transpired at work. If it was a pressing concern, then we would make an exception, but these were rare. Instead, we made the decision to make appointments during work hours to discuss issues affecting our business.

Will continued being concerned about the business and how disorganized everything seemed. He was limited in his ability to handle operations as he still had to see patients at the clinic and the local children's hospital. His primary role was that of clinician and he could not relinquish his role because he was the highest producing dentist and we could not afford for him to step away from seeing patients.

Although I had business experience running my pharmacy and was engaged in mergers and acquisitions with the leadership team at Target, I had no idea how to run a multi-location dental business. This was beyond my scope of competence, and I did not feel comfortable in this role. I also did not understand the intricacies involved in a dental business. For example, compliance issues, legal considerations, work flows, etc. were all foreign to me. I knew I was not the right person for this job and did not want to carry this type of responsibility any longer. Will agreed as well, and he also felt that assigning an operations role to me would be detrimental to our personal relationship, since it would cause unnecessary stress and tension in our marriage.

When Will asked for my opinion on promoting his dental assistant to the role of operations director, I expressed my belief that she would be a suitable candidate. I observed that she had a likable personality and appeared to have a good understanding of dentistry. Additionally, she demonstrated initiative and was not afraid to speak up when something prompted our attention. These qualities led us to believe that she had the potential to excel in a leadership position.

A few days later, after carefully considering our decision, Will and I approached her and offered her the promotion. She was overjoyed and expressed her gratitude for the opportunity. Personally, I felt a sense of relief knowing that we had made a decision that would benefit both our business and our marriage.

Chapter Sixteen

Ally's Promotion

William Peña

I N A DENTAL BUSINESS, running one or two offices is somewhat manageable for the dentist-owner to operate. It is usually around opening the third office that things become a bit chaotic. It is at this point that having proper oversight, the right staff, and efficient systems and processes are most critical. After opening our third office in 2015, we figured that we needed a designated person who would manage the operations of the business.

A dental assistant that worked with me at the time (that we shall name "Ally" to safeguard her anonymity) demonstrated a willingness to run the business operations for us. She was respectful, supportive, and well liked by her peers. She also displayed initiative and showed sanguine passion for our company's mission and purpose. So, we decided to promote her to director of operations—a position that entailed oversight of the office managers and production, as well as oversight of hiring and termination of employees, etc. Initially, she performed relatively well and demonstrated seemingly great aptitude in her role.

Grand opening of our 3ʳᵈ location in Coral Springs, Florida.

Then when we opened our corporate office and our fourth dental office in 2016, it was like the wind had exited her sails, and she began to falter in her role of managing the company's operations. We began to notice a lack of uniform processes and inadequate staff training. Richelle and I would do our office visits and ask random team members what their roles and responsibilities were. They would give us a blank "deer-in-headlights" stare; they were utterly clueless as to what their job entailed!

When we asked the office managers how to perform basic managerial tasks, the universal answer seemed to be, "I just call Ally whenever I don't know how to do something, and she does it for me." On numerous occasions, we brought our concerns to Ally, especially the lack of training and absence of uniform procedures at the offices. Ally would promise us that she would start delegating tasks to her direct reports and refrain from being the "mother hen" of her team, solving every single problem they encountered at work.

She also came up with the idea of creating operating manuals that would describe how each of the core tasks of the offices was properly performed, and after finishing these training manuals, she told me she would host training sessions with the office managers. We thought it was a good plan and encouraged her to proceed with the initiative.

In meeting after meeting, I would ask to see the manuals, and Ally would give me the usual litany of excuses as to why the manuals remained unfinished—she was busy training one of the office managers, she was preoccupied with a pressing issue with a dental provider, she was solving a problem at one of the offices, etc. In the meantime, team members at the offices continued to work without knowing what their exact roles were and without any guidance whatsoever. Eventually, these employees grew frustrated with our lack of progress in demonstrating improvements and became disgruntled. One by one, these employees began resigning from their positions.

Employee morale and office performance at this time suffered and was at an all-time low. Things got so bad that I received a call from a fellow pediatric dentist, one of our local competitors, telling me that she was "concerned" because so many of our former employees were resigning and she was put in the "difficult" position of having to hire them. I explained that we were simply undergoing a period of growing pains. Then thanked her for the call and for her concern and hung up the phone.

We had work to do.

After that phone call, we confronted Ally once again about the high employee turnover in our business. Initially, she became defensive and began offering excuses to justify the exodus of team members.

We were not buying into her justifications any longer, and at this point, she relented and admitted that she was a bit "lost" and felt overwhelmed with her responsibilities as the operations director. Moreover, she said, she needed "extra training" in the area of leadership. Since it was our philosophy to treat our team members well and because Ally had such a great attitude and predisposition, we went to the extent of paying for her to obtain a master's in business administration and also enrolled her in numerous leadership courses. We were optimistic that these tools would better equip her for the tasks at hand. Unfortunately, none of those initiatives worked, and the same issues continued to plague our company.

Chaos began to ensue throughout the organization. Ally was constantly preoccupied with putting out fires, and she neglected to oversee the performance of the office managers. Since there was no accountability whatsoever, the office managers did not take the initiative to fill the schedules. There was absolutely no sense of urgency. Since the office schedules were not full and our overhead expenses were so high, we began to lose money. The high turnover with our team members also affected us, since it took money and time (two precious resources that were scarce at the time) to hire and train new team members.

We finally realized that no matter how hard we tried to help Ally grow in her role as the operations director, she unfortunately did not have the skillset and would never rise to be the leader we wanted, or needed, her to be. We knew that if we wanted to continue growing the business and further expand our footprint with more offices in different communities, her lack of operational and leadership acumen would hinder our ambitions.

Richelle and I sat down one day after work and had an extensive conversation about what to do with Ally. We were facing a dilemma because we knew that she meant well and that her heart was in the right place. We honestly thought that she had tried her best, but unfortunately she was not the right person to lead our operations. Her lack of experience in managing work flows, we believed, was a significant factor in her not performing well in her role. She ultimately did not have the knowledge or the experience to carry out her tasks and lead her team. It was a difficult decision, but we decided that parting ways with Ally would be in the company's best interest.

The question then was who would take her place. In the end, Richelle and I both decided that I would be the best person to take over the operations role. We agreed that as the leader of the company with the ability to make more effective high-level decisions, I should be intimately involved in its operations. The other factor was that we were also losing money, so we couldn't afford to hire a professional manager. It was a daunting realization because although I understood dentistry from a clinical perspective, I only had a limited purview of its operations.

It's interesting to note that although the majority of dentists are small-business owners, we are provided with minimal training in business or practice management. The focus of our education in dental school primarily revolves around the technical aspects of our profession and theoretical knowledge through research.

Despite my shortcomings running an organization, I had to now step up and lead our business to success. No pressure!

Chapter Seventeen

Waiting Too Long

Richelle Peña

DEALING WITH THE DIFFICULTIES with Ally and then Will taking over as director of operations taught us important things. First, we learned from our experience with our former operations director that you can delegate responsibilities to team members, but you have to be keenly aware of their decision-making and the impact those decisions are having on the performance and, ultimately, the profitability of your business.

Although we were aware of what Ally was doing, in hindsight we should have taken action sooner and taken over the reins of the business a lot quicker. Instead, we gave her the benefit of the doubt, continued to believe in her, and watched our business crumble.

Furthermore, to maximize the performance of your organization, it is imperative that you hire people for a particular role that already have the requisite skills and later help them adapt those skills to your business. Trying to teach someone with no job-related experience or knowledge the skills necessary to perform their job is a sure recipe for disaster, especially if it is an important role in an evolving and complex business.

Our experiences with Ally are also a great example of one of our guiding principles, *hire for attitude; train for skill.* You cannot bring someone with a great attitude that has limited or no aptitude for the role you are either hiring or promoting them for. They must already have a certain amount of experience and skill for the job or role you are assigning them; otherwise, you are setting that person up for failure. The candidate must have a great attitude *and* aptitude for the job, with attitude slightly outweighing the person's job-related expertise.

In retrospect, we should have promoted Ally to a less grueling and demanding role (such as an office manager) and then slowly trained her for the role of operations director. But honestly—and by no means is this an excuse or justification—we were learning the business side ourselves and were not equipped to make that type of inference at that point in our career.

After parting ways with Ally and taking over her role as operations director, Will needed to quickly learn how to perform dutifully in his new position. The problem was he had never run an organization, as he had not held a position like this in the past. Moreover, he had limited time because he worked in the clinic six days per week. Where was he going to find the time to see patients in the clinic *and* handle the company's operations?

Naturally, he was intimidated and nervous.

Looking back on this period, we both realized that the reason why we held on to Ally for so long, despite her lackluster performance, was because we knew deep down that if we parted ways with her, we would have no suitable replacement. As Will mentioned, the company at the time could not afford a professional manager, and we did not want to hire someone with an unproven track record. Therefore, the responsibility fell squarely on Will, as the leader, to push outside his comfort zone and put his leadership skills to the test to protect our company from further damage. He will share his experiences on becoming an operations leader in the next chapter.

Based on my areas of expertise and my proven track record in patient procurement, I decided to take on the role of director of corporate development, a position that entailed not only marketing and public relations, but also the responsibility of running our new call center. Will and I both thought that running the call center was a good fit for me because this was the funnel where all new patients that had heard about us through my various marketing campaigns would first interact with our business. I wanted to control this aspect of the business because I wanted a patient's first interaction with our business to be overwhelmingly positive. Therefore, part of my job was to train my new team on proper phone etiquette. I emphasized various key performance measures such as missed call rates, outbound and inbound call duration, etc., but my primary focus was customer service.

I would remind my team, "Smile. They can hear it in your voice," and constantly train them on proper phone etiquette. Then I would monitor their calls and provide feedback on areas where I felt they could improve. If a call center representative was not kind or did not demonstrate empathy to a parent on a call, I would remind them of the purpose of our business. Since we dealt extensively with parents of children with special needs, I taught my team how to ask certain questions so as to not offend the parent. For example, instead of simply asking, "Does your child have special needs?" they would be instructed to ask, "Does your child require any special accommodations or have a medical condition that we should be aware of?" We wanted to collect pertinent patient information, but we wanted to do so in a tactful and compassionate manner.

It was a learning experience, as I had never run a call center. It was challenging and required a lot of trial and error, but what made it easier for me was knowing my objective—providing an exceptional experience to all our new patients calling our office. Because of this, I could work backward and figure out how I wanted to train my team to accomplish this goal.

I took enormous satisfaction knowing that I was able to have a positive impact on someone's day simply by the way they were greeted when they called our offices. I enjoyed my new role, but I was worried about how Will was faring in his new role as operations director.

Despite the challenges we faced with Ally's promotion, I found comfort in the fact that I had the foresight to recognize my limitations and refrain from taking on a role that I was neither qualified nor passionate about. Had I formally taken on the operations role, I believe I would have encountered similar difficulties as Ally, leading to frequent arguments between Will and me. This could have potentially strained our working relationship and jeopardized our ability to collaborate effectively.

Reflecting on this situation, I am grateful that I trusted my intuition and passed the operations role to someone else. This decision allowed me to focus on areas where I could contribute effectively and maintain my confidence in myself. I believe that God guided me in making this choice, protecting our partnership and preserving our ability to work together harmoniously.

Throughout the challenges we faced with Ally and the issues plaguing our company, Will and I relied on each other for advice and guidance. I provided a different perspective for him to consider, offering insights and suggestions. Together, we weathered the storm and emerged stronger as a team. I started to realize our strength in unity as a married couple building something that we both could control.

Looking back, I am grateful for the lessons learned and the growth we experienced as a result of these challenges. They shaped us into more resilient and adaptable entrepreneurs, ready to face whatever obstacles may come our way.

Chapter Eighteen

A Leader is Born

William Peña

As RICHELLE MENTIONED IN the previous chapter, I am grateful that she did not take on the operations role. It would have been detrimental to our partnership as business owners and as a married couple. Instead, Richelle excelled in her role as the director of corporate development. Her marketing efforts successfully attracted a significant number of patients to our offices, and her leadership with the call center team greatly enhanced the patient experience.

I was relieved to see Richelle thriving in a role that she was passionate about. It is crucial to find fulfillment in the work we do, as forcing oneself to perform tasks that are dreaded can lead to burnout and subpar results. Seeing how Richelle had stepped outside her comfort zone and taken on her new role in full stride (with amazing results) inspired me to do the same in my new role as operations director.

Assuming the role, however, was a significant undertaking, as it required me to curtail my clinical responsibilities to accommodate my managerial duties. After considering the financial impact of truncating my clinical schedule with Richelle, we decided arbitrarily that I should have two days per week to carry out my administrative tasks. Given the amount of work that needed to be done, two days was insufficient time to properly handle the operations, and I had to learn to be extremely efficient with my time. I promoted a dental assistant that had leadership potential to be my operations coordinator. This role entailed executing any operational initiatives and changes that Richelle and I deemed necessary, and also overseeing the office managers. This helped alleviate some of my time constraints.

To be effective in my new role, however, I needed to immerse myself into the business to properly learn how the company functioned from an operations perspective.

During my administrative time, I had to familiarize myself with the day-to-day operations of our offices. I also needed to learn the various processes and systems in place, from scheduling appointments to managing our supply inventory. Lastly, I needed to work closely with our team members to get their input and feedback on how we could improve efficiency and enhance the patient experience.

I knew that by taking on the operations role I would have a broader perspective on our business as a whole. I would be able to identify areas where we could streamline processes, reduce costs, and improve overall performance. This knowledge would empower me to make strategic decisions that would benefit our business in the long run.

Although I knew that assuming this role would provide me valuable insights into the challenges and opportunities within our operations, I felt an enormous pressure to perform once I formally stepped into my new position.

In 2016, the company was in complete disarray, and we were hemorrhaging money. I was stressed knowing that I not only had to learn the operations role, but I had to master it in a relatively short amount of time in order to turn around the company. To circumvent my lack of operational experience, however, I leaned on the lessons that I had learned early on in my life. I realized that the first thing I had to do was quiet the noise and negative chatter of my mind. I could not think properly if my mind was in a frazzled or panicked state. Next, I needed to create a cohesive, well-thought-out plan to address the primary issues plaguing the business. Once I identified the issues, I could then create a road map to help me solve each of the company's issues and, in turn, ensure a positive turnaround.

The business was in a state of chaos—patient reviews were trending negative, our staff morale was at an all-time low, and our expenses were too high, so we were losing a large amount of money.

The first thing I did was perform a 360-degree survey with all employees and managers to get their feedback on their roles and responsibilities. I also did an audit of the physical state of the offices to assess cleanliness, pending repairs, etc. I also personally observed core processes being carried out by team members, and spoke with patients to get their feedback on their experience at the offices. From the results of these surveys and my own observations, I put together an action plan to get the offices in an optimal operational condition.

From the survey, I learned what I already intuitively knew. Employees did not receive any training, did not have performance reviews, did not understand their roles and responsibilities, etc.

From my interactions with team members and my own assessment at each office, I created operational manuals with step-by-step descriptions and detailed illustrations of every core process, from how to properly greet and check in a patient to how to submit insurance claims once the patient was seen. Along with these, I also added protocols with management's expectations of employees and ongoing training programs for new and existing team members. Biannual performance reviews were also introduced. These reviews helped provide feedback to employees on how well they were performing and areas of opportunity. Lastly, I created much-needed accountability systems. Depending on the task, I would conduct periodic audits to evaluate compliance in different areas of the business, such as scheduling, confirmations, etc.

Since the company as a whole was losing money, I decided to pump the brakes on our growth plans and focus instead on achieving individual office profitability rather than trying to increase our office count.

Thanks to Richelle, who oversaw our marketing programs, we increased both our marketing campaigns and our community relations efforts. She strategically placed ads in print magazines geared toward children and families. She also began leveraging social media and advertising on various platforms with targeted ads, as well as continuing her grassroots efforts and signing up for community events and school presentations. She even planned an extraordinary patient appreciation event at a local theater to thank our patients for their continued loyalty to our business.

Slowly, our operations began turning around and our business began to stabilize. Our company now had a well-trained team, clearly defined roles and responsibilities, proper systems and processes, and auditing checklists in place. As a result, we were once again growing our revenues and generating a profit.

I am grateful for the guidance and wisdom that I received from God, which allowed me to learn and understand the operations of our business in a relatively short amount of time. This divine illumination enabled me to navigate through the complexities and challenges of the role with ease and efficiency, and we were able to execute an effective turnaround. It was stressful, and the results were not immediate; it took us nearly eighteen months to see any positive results. But at least we knew that we would once again survive as a business.

It is also worth mentioning that the rollercoaster journey of our business undeniably had an impact on our personal lives. Our emotions were tethered to the ups and downs of our business, and the stress often spilled over into our family life. However, we found ways to cope with the challenges and maintain a sense of balance.

One of the ways we managed the stress was through travel. As our children grew older, we took advantage of every opportunity to go on trips during holidays, breaks, and birthdays. These family getaways provided us with much-needed respite from the stress of running our business and allowed us to create cherished memories together. Although we were extremely busy at work, creating proper systems and implementing processes, we made time to spend with our family. The time spent away from the demands of our business helped us recharge and rejuvenate, and also bond as a family. The way we see it, work will never cease to exist but your time with your family is limited. Once the kids grow up (especially when they start attending college), they have an increasing amount of responsibility (school work, extracurricular activities, etc.) that consumes their free time, leaving less opportunities to connect with parents on a more frequent basis.

In addition to family travel, Richelle and I made it a priority to continue with our date nights. These moments allowed us to focus on nurturing our marriage and strengthening our bond. We recognized the importance of maintaining a strong partnership, especially during times of stress and uncertainty. Date nights provided us with an opportunity to talk about non-work related things and helped us reconnect.

To this day, I continue to look forward to traveling with my family and spending quality time with Richelle on our date nights. These activities serve as anchors in my life, helping me stay grounded amidst the challenges and demands of running our business. They remind me of the importance of prioritizing our family and personal well-being, in alignment with our G.F.B Principle.

By finding ways to alleviate the pressures of our business and prioritize our family and relationship, we were able to navigate the rollercoaster ride with resilience and maintain a sense of calm and balance in our lives.

Chapter Nineteen

Whiskey and Vallenatos

William Peña

D URING THOSE STRESSFUL AND scary moments after I took over the operations role, I would lean heavily not just on Richelle, but on my father as well. I consider him to this day as my life and business advisor, since he has been a small-business owner for over four decades. Even though my father has an irascible personality, I love talking to him because he is brutally honest and will provide his opinions, even if they are unsolicited. He is also like me in so many ways. We have the same taste in music, food, and have similar worldviews.

Over glasses of Macallan whiskey and *vallenato* music, he would remind me of the importance of maintaining "balance" in one's life. He noticed my ambition and my plans to open more offices despite the incredible stress of running our existing locations, and he was rightfully concerned. I would futilely try and reassure him, "Don't worry, *papi*, I can handle the pressure. Besides, we've had incredible success with our business thus far and there's so much left for us to do. We have to continue taking advantage of the opportunities that are constantly presenting themselves. I can build a large, nationwide company *and* make time for Richelle and the kids."

I realized now that I was in a state of denial, or perhaps I was delusional. A part of me, driven by my idealistic nature, harbored a strong desire to continue expanding our business and establish a vast network of offices. However, deep down, a more realistic side of me subconsciously cautioned against pursuing this ambitious goal. I was aware, on some level, that maintaining a healthy work-life balance while building such an empire would be a significant challenge.

My dad knew better. Being wise and perceptive, he recognized this internal struggle within me. Instead of outright telling me that my aspirations were unrealistic, he employed a more subtle approach. He would drop innuendos and make thought-provoking comments that encouraged me to consider the long-term implications of my goals. By doing so, he gently nudged me toward a more balanced perspective.

He would often ask me during our late-night talks, "Willy, how many offices will you *eventually* open?" and I would respond, "I don't know. I could open ten or perhaps a hundred offices. I have to take advantage of the fact that our banks are lending money to us to open up more offices and there's tremendous opportunities in other markets!"

He then poignantly told me, "*Papito*, you know that there will come a point in your career when you will have to choose between running your company and being present with your family, especially as the company continues to grow. You will see that eventually the demands of the business will become so overwhelming that you will inevitably have to dedicate more time to it. Don't get to that point, because you will regret missing the milestones of my grandchildren and precious time with your family, and from what I know, that is extremely important to you."

I will admit that I do not listen or take advice from many people, but the opinions and lessons given to me by my father are not only highly valued and appreciated, but also weigh heavily on my soul. During our conversations, I would never argue or get defensive with my father. I would simply listen and try to assimilate the sage advice being given to me from a man I respect so much. I appreciated my father's approach, as it allowed me to come to my own realizations and conclusions. Being someone who generally dislikes being told what to do, his indirect guidance was more effective in helping me reassess my long-term goals and priorities.

My father played a crucial role in keeping me grounded during that period of my life. Our conversations served as a reality check, forcing me to confront the impact that my growing entrepreneurial ambitions were having on my personal life. His guidance and concern made me pause and reflect on my long-term goals and the viability of pursuing an aggressive expansion plan.

I kept asking myself, *Can I truly grow the company, have offices in different states, and still make time for my wife and kids?* Perhaps because of my ego, my idealistic nature, or my unwavering commitment to my original vision for the business, I had convinced myself that I was capable of accomplishing my lofty ambitions. Slowly, however, my father's warnings began occupying space in my mind and I began the process of reevaluating my professional objectives.

Despite my internal struggles, I kept up the facade of enthusiasm, both to my team and to myself. I felt that admitting my true feelings would be tantamount to failure, a betrayal of the ambitious image I had projected. This internal conflict led to increased anxiety and constant rumination, further exacerbating my stress levels.

During this time, I found myself caught in a web of conflicting emotions. On one hand, I was thrilled with our achievements and the growth we were experiencing. The prospect of expanding our company and reaching new heights filled me with excitement and confidence. However, on the other hand, I was grappling with the prospect of becoming so involved with the business that it would leave me no time for my personal life.

As my father had warned me, the demands of a growing business were increasing exponentially. The more successful we became, the more time and energy it required. I was determined not to let these demands interfere with my family life, so I tried to delegate tasks and manage my time more efficiently in order to meet my personal commitments. I was determined not to miss one of my kid's activities or a date night with Richelle.

But the constant juggling act eventually took a toll on me. I was constantly on the move, trying to fulfill both my professional and personal responsibilities. The pressure I put on myself to never miss a moment with my children or neglect my responsibilities at work was overwhelming. I was stretched thin and exhausted, both physically and mentally.

During periods when the business faced challenges and setbacks, my doubts and insecurities would resurface. I questioned whether I could sustain this lifestyle in the long run. The constant stress and self-doubt began to affect my health and well-being. I was caught in a cycle of suppressing my own emotions and pushing myself to the limit, all in the pursuit of being a successful businessman and a devoted father.

I contemplated the sustainability of my current lifestyle and recognized that a decision needed to be made. As an entrepreneur, I was driven by the desire to continue growing our business and taking on new challenges. However, as a family man, I understood the importance of being present for my loved ones and not sacrificing precious time with them.

After careful consideration and heartfelt discussions with my wife, Richelle, we came to a mutual decision.

Chapter Twenty

Being at a Crossroads

Richelle Peña

I KNEW THAT WILL had a lot on his mind, and I was growing concerned about his mental and emotional wellbeing. His demeanor had changed, and he appeared constantly preoccupied and afflicted. Despite his efforts to masquerade his true feelings from the children, I could sense the weight of his responsibilities and the immense pressure he was under at work. Taking on the operations role had been a significant challenge for him, as he had to quickly learn and adapt to a completely new set of responsibilities. He had made promises to his team to bring about positive change in the company, and the burden of fulfilling those promises weighed heavily on him.

In addition, he found himself at a crossroads, torn between two possible paths for the company. On one hand, he could opt to continue managing our existing offices and not growing the company any further. This would provide us stability and allow us to focus on maintaining and optimizing the existing operations. On the other hand, he could push forward with his expansion plans, setting aside his own uncertainties and embracing the potential growth opportunities.

During numerous conversations, Will shared with me his uncertainty about how to proceed with the company. His dilemma and internal anguish were evidently causing him significant distress.

As his wife and business partner, I offered him arguments for both options, understanding the importance of considering various perspectives. I told him that I would be supportive in whatever he ultimately decided, but he needed to properly reflect on what truly mattered to him, both personally and professionally, and make a decision. I encouraged him to consider his long-term goals, the impact on our family life, and the alignment with his core values.

I knew that making such a decision was not easy, but I made it a priority to be there for him and provide him with an emphatic ear. He would often seek comfort in our conversations, appreciating my ability to see the positive in every situation and my unwavering optimism. While I may not have had all the answers or a solution to his dilemma, I at least offered him my support and understanding.

To be honest, considering Will's emotional state at the time, I was convinced that he would refrain from further expanding our company. However, I wouldn't know for certain until we spoke and he shared his renewed vision with me. Witnessing Will's inner turmoil and the burden of dealing with numerous significant issues filled me with fear and concern for his well-being. When you are with someone for so long, and in addition to being married, you are also professionally intertwined, you begin assimilating and internalizing their emotions.

As I always do during the difficult periods of my life, I lean heavily on my faith. I understand that the challenges we face are lessons that God puts on our lives for a reason. If we overcome them, then we will significantly grow as a person. As pastor Joel Osteen states, "A setback is a setup for a stronger comeback." Nonetheless, going through these tribulations can be downright scary.

I wasn't entirely sure what lesson Will, and by extension, I, would learn from this situation, but rather than get discouraged (or freak out), I chose to adopt a "fake it until I make it" mindset. My main focus became being a pillar of strength for my husband and our family. When you and your spouse work together, it's crucial that one of you remain calm and composed while the other may be overwhelmed. Our strength derived from our mutual support and commitment to one another; whenever one of us faltered, the other was there to provide encouragement.

This symbiotic relationship is one of the remarkable advantages of working alongside Will. In a conventional workplace, a leader cannot openly confide in a colleague about their true emotions. Such vulnerability could have detrimental effects on the business and the leader's credibility, ultimately eroding the team's trust.

After some time, Will finally asked to speak with me to discuss our company's future plans. When he finally revealed his plan to me, I was taken aback and filled with disbelief.

Will told me that after contemplating the issue numerous times, he had come to the conclusion that we should continue expanding the business! I couldn't help but stare at my husband, my mind racing to process the unexpected turn of events. His proposal had caught me completely off guard, leaving me speechless and bewildered. As I tried to regain my composure, my face must have betrayed my astonishment. Sensing my confusion, Will swiftly shifted his stance, his eyes filled with determination. He understood the need to clarify his proposition further, realizing that his initial explanation had left me in a state of shock and disbelief. He offered to delve into the intricate details, hoping to alleviate any doubts or uncertainties that lingered in my mind.

Before he could elaborate, however, I asked him with evident ire and frustration in my voice, "You want to continue growing the business despite feeling stressed and mentally fatigued? Are you sure this is what you want? Can you handle the pressure of opening more offices with all the managerial complexities that these entail? You said that opening more offices would ultimately affect your time at home with the kids and now you are proposing to continue with your aggressive expansion plans?"

Will calmly replied, "Richelle, you know that my priority will always be my family. I never want to sacrifice my time with you and the kids to continue growing our business. I decided not to pursue an ambitious national expansion, but I do want to grow our business just a bit more."

After my initial shock wore off, I asked him to further elaborate on his plans as I was still vexed. Will explained to me that he wanted to open just five to seven *additional* locations over the course of the next decade. Will explained that all the offices would be in the south Florida area, so they were geographically close and he wouldn't need to travel and be away from us.

He also rationalized that the most stressful and time-consuming part of opening offices was the usual twelve-month ramp up period when we had to actively market our services to new patients. Once an office was established, however, we "only" had to deal with the day-to-day issues that usually arose, but these were at least not as daunting as the stress of potentially running out of money during the initial phase because there were not enough patients. Besides, he explained, once our company's growth had subsided, he would take a step back and hire or promote someone to manage the operations of the business further alleviating the pressure on him.

For reasons unbeknownst to me, Will had completely downplayed the extremely difficult task of opening up a dental office from scratch and managing the operations. I felt that by doing so, Will was invalidating the way he was feeling. I personally thought that his new plan, although curtailed significantly from the original, was still a major undertaking. We would essentially be tripling the size of our current company within a ten-year span.

I asked him, now more calmly, "Why are you so adamant on pursuing this new plan for the company? I honestly thought that you were going to tell me that you were going to abandon your expansion plans and simply manage the offices we already have. I assumed that perhaps you would also eventually relinquish your clinical duties entirely so you can just dedicate yourself to overseeing the operations and not be so overwhelmed." I then shared the way I was feeling with him, "Will, I'm honestly concerned for you. You are always on the move, jumping from one thing to the next. I'm scared of something happening to you because of the immense pressure you place on yourself."

He answered, "I understand your concern for the way I'm feeling, but it is important for me to fulfill the commitments I made to you before we started our business. I promised you financial freedom so that we can accomplish our dreams and I intend to come true on my word." He then attempted to further explain his plans, "I did the calculation and having an organization with eight to ten offices would generate enough money to maintain our lifestyle, buy our dream home, and pay for our children's college education." Then he ended his impassioned plea with, "Don't worry, knowing our endgame gives me clarity of what I need to focus on. I won't allow the stress or pressure to get to me because I know that in a few years, I will not be actively managing the business."

In all honesty, I was cynical of Will's proposal and wondered if it was a pipe dream. But, he had apparently done his homework and he seemed confident that he could successfully execute his plan and still maintain balance.

I then asked Will what had made him reconsider his plans for nationwide expansion. He told me, "Richelle, opening a vast network of offices across the country would require us to seek financial partners who would utilize our existing business platform to drive aggressive expansion. They would provide the financial resources and the operational expertise to grow, but it would come at a steep cost—control. By having a private equity firm as a business partner, we will be beholden to their expectations for growth and they may have us run the business differently in order for us to meet their financial objectives. The price that I would have to personally pay in terms of time away from my family and the managerial stress is too great, and I will not acquiesce to that sort of deal. I want us to own our business in its entirety so that we can continue making decisions that are in our best interest."

Similar to my husband, I did not want a bunch of suits calling the shots. It would be like having a boss again and we both definitely did not want that.

I was still unsure if we could sustain Will's proposed level of growth for the company and continue maintaining balance, but I knew that he would personally scale back our expansion plans if he felt that the business was interfering with our family time. One great thing about Will is that although he oftentimes has idealistic and grandiose aspirations, he can also be realistic and would not hesitate to dial back his plans if they go against his vision for his life and his core values.

I also admire and respect my husband's willingness to sacrifice everything to honor his promises and commitments. His integrity is awe-inspiring, but I was constantly concerned that his relentless pursuit of his goals would have deleterious effects on his mental and physical health.

Although I was skeptical with his future vision for the company, I decided to support Will's plan. He seemed convinced that we could accomplish it and at least it seemed to be more achievable than our original one.

In retrospect, I should've pushed back on his plan a lot harder and offered a varying perspective to convince Will to reconsider. Deep down, I knew that his goals were not feasible based on what he wanted to accomplish personally. I knew that he was being quixotic and that eventually the pressure of running the business and trying to be a super dad were going to catch up with him.

Chapter Twenty-One

Finding Balance

Richelle Peña

ALTHOUGH I HAD CLARITY on our endgame, I remained concerned about the viability of Will's plans. I felt even more distressed because I was starting to feel overwhelmed as our company started to expand. Similar to Will, I was striving to find a balance between my professional responsibilities, being a mother, and prioritizing my own well-being.

One of the advantages of my role as director of corporate development, however, was that I had a flexible schedule. I had properly trained my call center team and appointed one of my best performers as their lead. This alleviated a lot of time on my schedule. I could now do my work and plan my activities based around my kids' schedules.

I finally had the opportunity to spend more time with our children, and I took full advantage of it. I was now able to take them to school and pick them up. I was also able to take them to their extra-curricular activities and have playdates with other moms from their school. It was a wonderful experience for me as a mom.

In retrospect, although the children were too young to remember, I struggled with feelings of "mom guilt" and felt the need to compensate for what I believed was lost time. I had to constantly remind myself that the significance lies not in the amount of time spent with my children, but in the *quality of the time* spent with them. Even though I wasn't a stay-at-home mom during their formative years, I still made a deliberate effort to be present for them after work, particularly during meals and all their school functions.

Despite the joy I felt at finally having time for my children, I also needed to dedicate time to continue overseeing my duties at work and helping Will manage the business. Eventually, the myriad of commitments really began taking a toll on me. I am not one to complain or show weakness, but at that time, I was feeling distraught and fatigued. I was handling a lot and began to sense that I had no real outlet. While I initially turned to fitness classes to shed the baby weight, the mounting work stress made me realize I needed something more.

Then one day, out of the blue, my sister-in-law, Nicole, asked Will and me, "Hey, do you guys want to run a half-marathon with me?"

"Definitely not!" I immediately replied. At the time, I did not consider myself an athlete, much less a runner. Will replied, "Um . . . hell no. Only crazy people run for hours on end."

Despite our immediate refusal, we did give it some more thought. We were both terrified of the idea of running so many miles and having only three months to train for the event. What made matters worse was that we had no idea what to expect since we had never participated in an endurance event. We would be truly trekking in uncharted territory, and naturally, it made us nervous and apprehensive.

I was also thirty-four years old at the time and thought that I was too old to start marathon training. I kept asking myself, *What if I fail? What if I am too slow? What if I pass out? What will people think if I don't make it to the finish line?* All these "what if's" passed through my mind, and I'm sure similar thoughts were running through Will's head (no pun intended). It was as if my mind was trying to stop me from doing something that was challenging.

Eventually, we both accepted the challenge. I personally wanted to prove to myself that I could do anything I put my mind to. I knew that once I started pushing myself outside my comfort zone and actually succeeded, I would build my confidence and mindset. Besides, Will was also doing the race with me, and we could spend quality time training together. Fortunately, my parents and Will's dad agreed to take turns and watch the kids while we went out for our long training runs, which usually took place on Saturday mornings.

Training started during the month of October when the weather was a bit more pleasant compared to the usual heat and humidity characteristic of south Florida. We had a training plan, we were motivated, and more importantly, we had each other.

We eventually ran that half-marathon and completed it in a decent time. I even beat Will! I was amazed at how well my body responded to the training. More importantly, I was shocked at my level of endurance. I never thought I could accomplish a running event such as the half-marathon, but I did it because I did not let fear dictate what I could or should do. I chose to step outside my comfort zone, and because I did, I discovered that I am, in fact, a runner.

13.1 Fort Lauderdale Half-Marathon

Running then became a huge part of our lives and a great way for us to relieve the stress we were experiencing at work. Since we could not leave the kids alone, we would take turns running outside, or one of us would run on our treadmill at home while the other went for an outdoor run. On those weekends when our parents were available to babysit, Will and I would go on a run together. It was a wonderful way to bond and spend time with one another doing something that was beneficial to our overall health.

If I was worried about something or had anxiety regarding a work-related issue, I would go for a run to clear my head. The rush of dopamine—the so-called "runner's high"—is a great way to feel better despite the difficulties that you are facing in your life. I became a better entrepreneur because running offered me an escape—a relief—from my everyday stresses of managing a business and a home, and I am eternally grateful that my sister-in-law introduced me to running.

Aside from my training runs in preparation for the Miami Half-Marathon, I also joined a Pure Barre studio near my house and attended classes three to four times a week. Barre is a full-body workout that focuses on low-impact, small movements that strengthen and tone your body. I wanted a workout that would make me feel good and that would challenge me with calisthenics to gain strength and to help me regain my pre-mommy body, and I had found it. I fell in love from the first day of class and became addicted. It was also a good complement to running.

I planned my workouts early in the morning so they didn't affect my work or my duties as a mom. You can make time for anything that is important to you, and every entrepreneur and parent should, in my humble opinion, prioritize working out and cardiovascular exercise to improve their health and overall wellbeing.

At one point, I came to the realization that in the years before running our first half-marathon I was so focused on my children and the business that I failed to properly focus on *myself.*

I had neglected my physical health. Thankfully, I ate a balanced diet and did not gain too much weight, but I still felt weak and unenergetic.

I unintentionally overlooked my friendships as well. Before starting my entrepreneurial journey with Will, I made sure to schedule regular meet-ups with my friends, even if it was for a brief encounter to grab coffee. I cherish my moments with my girlfriends, as it allows us to have meaningful conversations, have fun, and strengthen our bond. However, the demands of motherhood and running a business resulted in less time spent with them. This realization saddened me, as I understood that our busy lives of building a business and raising a family left little time for personal relationships.

That all changed with that race. I realized that if I did not exercise and take care of myself—and make time for those things that are important to me, such as creating memories with my girlfriends—then I would not be fully happy as an individual and could also succumb to possible physical and mental ailments in the future. I made a choice to make fitness a normal part of my daily routine, and I have not stopped exercising and taking care of myself since running the Miami Half-Marathon in 2017.

I have also made spending time with my friends a personal priority, and I usually go on a girls' trip with my besties once per year. Will supports my trip with my friends, and he is actually happy when I spend time with them, as this allows him to spend one-on-one time with the kids. I also come back fulfilled from spending time with my lifelong friends (some of my friends I have known since I was five years old). This positive energy, in turn, makes our home more joyful.

To me, the secret formula to a successful home is: happy mom = happy family!

Now that I had created balance, I felt happier, stronger, and my mind felt more clear and calm. As former law professor and attorney, Michael Josephson, famously stated, "The choices you make in your life will make your life." I was fortunate to have made this choice at a critical juncture in our professional career, as things were about to spiral out of control.

Chapter Twenty-Two

Growing Pains

William Peña

As the leader of the company, I felt a deep sense of responsibility to ensure its continuous growth and success. I placed immense expectations on myself to carefully oversee our operations and finances, especially during challenging periods. However, even when the business was doing well, a constant unease about the unknown future plagued my thoughts. *Would we have enough patients on the schedule? What if a dentist quits and we have to go through the extensive process of hiring another dentist? What if the Medicaid program decides to cut our rates?*

There were so many moving parts that I was constantly on edge. I was always worried about our team members, our business expenses, the Medicaid program (which accounted for a majority of our revenues), and even regulatory changes dictated by our governing bodies, such as the Board of Dentistry, OSHA, etc., that could severely affect our business.

I felt an enormous duty to my family, my team at work, to our patients, and to our banks. Our business needed to execute well and generate a profit. I also never wanted the soul of our company to disappear in the search of the almighty dollar. For me, it was a careful balancing act of staying true to our principles, but also meeting our financial expectations so we could continue operating and growing as a business. This pressure, no doubt, was oftentimes a lot to handle. In those difficult moments, I can see how entrepreneurs can turn to harmful ways to help them cope with the stressors from work. Alcohol, and even drugs, can be used to bring about brief moments of tranquility or euphoria during those difficult times.

I knew that this was not the route I wanted to take as it went against my personal code of ethics. Besides, what good would it do to pick up a bottle of alcohol and drink my problems away every night just because I was stressed? More importantly, what kind of an example would that be to my children? The only thing this would've done was lead me down a treacherous path of addiction and despair.

Instead, I turned to running thanks to Richelle's sister-in-law, Nicole. Running became my anxiolytic medicine of choice. It became almost an obsession for me. I would run five or six days weekly, always in pursuit of that runner's high. I ran that first half-marathon with Richelle and Nicole, and later ran dozens of half-marathons. Later, I leveled up to running full marathons. What is great about running is that I am able to do endurance events with Richelle, often engaging in friendly competition to see who could complete the course the fastest. We are also able to do our training runs together. This type of activity was not just a way to remain strong and healthy, but we also had the opportunity to spend quality time together.

It is great that my wife and I have so much in common and are able to do so many things together. It is reassuring to me that I have rarely endured difficult and terrifying moments in our business alone. Richelle has always been by my side, fighting alongside me.

I strongly believe that our business began to improve once I took up running as a way to cope with my stress and anxiety. The clarity that running brings me is unparalleled. When I run, I sleep better and feel more relaxed. It is an incredible feeling.

By early 2018, our company was performing well, and we were firing on all cylinders. We had once again resumed our growth, albeit slower and more strategic. We now had six offices under management, a corporate office, and I was more comfortable in my role as operations director and CEO of the company. Our team consisted of close to 120 team members, including 18 dentists and specialists. Our revenues were also topping the eight-figure-mark, a major milestone for our business.

Although I was happy with our company's performance, I remained cautiously optimistic during those moments when all seemed to be working well. Running a business is like riding a roller coaster. You have ups and downs, and sometimes you get swept sideways.

And sometimes the eerie silence that is felt when everything is going seemingly well in your business is a harbinger of impending doom.

Unfortunately, I would not be proven wrong.

For starters, Richelle and I took on a large amount of bank loans to acquire the real estate assets of our business, and to build and equip our dental offices. In addition to these loans, we took out lines of credit that we used as working capital to fund our business during periods of losses.

We also grew our administrative team significantly since 2016. We had anticipated a higher growth rate in our business (I will explain momentarily why our projected growth did not materialize), and we hired professionals to oversee legal, human resources, insurance, and IT. Because we had high debt levels and significant overhead expenses, we needed to operate near perfection to avoid generating losses. There was very little margin for error.

Many of our offices that we had opened in years prior had also reached a point of maturity where we could not further increase the number of patients seen. These offices had reached their capacity limit.

In other businesses, management will raise fees once a location has reached capacity. These price increases serve as a hedge against rising levels of inflation. At our company, however, we were not able to increase the fees for our services. This is because our largest payor, the children's Medicaid program administered by the State of Florida, did not grant fee increases on an annual basis (and they have not increased their fees in over a decade). Furthermore, we could not charge the patients anything that was not covered by Medicaid because it goes against their bylaws.

By 2019, we had been in business for almost eight years, and since we experienced rapid success early on, many new pediatric dentists began copying our business model, offering many of our same services and accepting most of the insurance plans that we took at our offices. We got into the market at the best time, but slowly the market started to change and become more saturated. Therefore, our competitive advantage slowly began eroding, and we did not experience the same demand for our services as we did when we first started. As a result, our growth began slowing and the company needed to spend way more in marketing to attract new patients.

All these changes meant that we had revenues that were not growing significantly year after year, but our expenses ballooned in that three-year period between 2016 and 2019. The result? Our profit margins shrank significantly, and we began losing money as a company once again.

I tried speaking with our insurance carriers to grant us a fee increase to no avail. We also tried adding complementary services that pair well with pediatric dentistry, such as oral surgery and orthodontics, but these initiatives ultimately failed and generated more losses for the company. Although these business lines were related to dental work, they had a certain business model that unfortunately fell outside our scope of knowledge.

Since I could not grow our revenues, I focused on reducing our expenses. All of our expenses were in line with industry benchmarks, with the exception of our payroll, our largest expense as a percentage of revenue. I reduced the salaries of our highest paid personnel—even reducing my own to zero for several months—and trimmed the number of team members at the offices, especially the ones that were underperforming. Many of our corporate team were shocked when the announcement was made to reduce salaries by fifteen percent, but they eventually understood the necessity of the decision. Our cost reduction efforts helped, but it was not enough, and we continued operating in the red.

Deep down, I knew that the administrative staff was our largest expense, but I preferred reducing their salaries rather than resorting to layoffs since I was so fond of our administrative team and their stellar performance. Over the years, they had contributed significantly to the company, adding value in areas such as compliance, hiring processes, and our IT infrastructure (which we relied heavily on to operate). I did not want to make a rash decision and terminate them. I figured that instead I would look at other areas of our business to save money. I reviewed our company's profit and loss statements, desperately trying to find other areas where I could reduce expenses, to no avail.

I was frustrated that we could not get our expenses under control despite the myriad of cost-reduction measures we had taken already.

I consulted with Richelle and shared how disappointed I was. We had done all that we possibly could, and perhaps the frustration I felt was clouding my mind and judgment. She, too, was baffled and could not think of any other ways to reduce our overhead expenses.

After we deliberated back and forth about how to solve the issues at our company and couldn't come up with a viable solution, we decided to bring in someone with a fresh perspective who could perhaps better orient us as to what needed to be done to finally get us profitable. We researched possible business consultants and hired one that had extensive experience working with large dental organizations such as ours.

Chapter Twenty-Three

Another Setback

Richelle Peña

DESPITE THE DESPERATE SITUATION our business was in, failure was never an option. More changes needed to be made in order to move the needle and finally become profitable. As Will mentioned, our revenues had been increasing year after year since we opened. Operationally though we were still losing money because of our high expenses.

We hired a consultant to review all of our company's financials and, after analyzing them, would provide recommendations on how to improve our business.

On a dreary, humid Friday morning in early November of 2019, Will and I were coming out of the gym when he abruptly stopped cold in his tracks while checking his phone. When I asked him why he had a solemn expression on his face, he mentioned that the consultant had just sent us an email containing his financial analysis of our company.

I checked the consultant's email as well, and my heart dropped as I saw the staggering losses generated by the company. I couldn't wrap my mind around the fact that we were once again in this terrible predicament. After all the hard work and streamlining that we had done, our company was on the brink of a financial crisis.

Will immediately called the consultant to speak about the terrible financial report. The consultant told us very candidly that given our "burn rate," meaning the money we were losing every week, we only had two months' worth of cash for expenses. Will and I were both terrified and devastated by this revelation, but there was no time for panic or self-pity. We needed to take action.

Before we could even ask, the consultant poignantly told us, "To save your company, you need to take more drastic measures. I know you made initial cuts to your payroll, but those cuts were not deep enough. You need to do more, and you need to do it fast. You are quickly running out of money. The deepest cuts you need to make are within your administrative team. Your corporate overhead is way too high."

Will and I needed time to process the consultant's recommendations. It was close to the holidays, and in order to save our company, we needed to part ways with people who had been good to us, were loyal to the company, and were extremely hardworking. It was one thing having to terminate someone for underperformance, but to do it out of sheer necessity or survival was something completely different.

Will, especially, took the news hard. He's a smart guy and intuitively knew that he had to lay off some of the administrative staff, even before we hired the consultant. He had told me many times that he preferred growing the business and increasing our revenues rather than having to resort to corporate layoffs, but ultimately, we were not able to. He figured that the consultant may show us a different way to save money, but instead he had arrived at the same conclusion that we already had.

One night after work, we stayed up late at home talking about what the consultant had recommended and what the next steps should be. This was a rare exception to our "no talking about work stuff at home" rule.

Will asked me, "What are your thoughts on what the consultant recommended?" I replied, "It seems as though we have no choice. I know you are hesitant, and trust me, I understand your pain, but ultimately we need to do what is best for our business, however difficult that decision may be." He replied with a grave expression, "Richelle, this is probably one of the hardest decisions I'll ever have to make. It's the holidays, and I honestly feel like the Grinch."

He was heartbroken knowing that he would have to deliver really bad news to some great individuals before the end of the year. And just a few days later, Will delivered the dreadful news to several administrative team members. He was shaken by the decisions he had made, and for a few days afterward, he remained out of sorts. Even though I was apprehensive and uncomfortable with the decisions that had to be made and the relationships that we had to sacrifice, I knew this needed to be done and stood by every decision that we ultimately had to make.

Although both Will and I were saddened by the decisions that were made, corporate restructurings happen all the time because as a business leader it's almost impossible to predict the future with any degree of certainty. You may have theories and may make assumptions based on available data and current market conditions, but macroeconomic factors—the state of the economy, inflation, politics, etc.—may completely derail even your best laid plans.

In the end, we had to close most administrative positions at the corporate level, including legal, human resources, IT, and our insurance department; we subsequently outsourced all these tasks to third parties. The only corporate positions left untouched were finance, operations, and marketing. The corporate building that we had purchased just a few years prior was also sold, and the few administrative support members that remained were asked to work from home.

Following the implementation of those cost-cutting measures, we were confident that our company would once again regain its profitability.

Throughout the process of restructuring, we were reminded of the importance of communication in order to avoid causing panic. We strongly believe in the notion that communication is an essential aspect of effective leadership, especially during times of crisis. During this difficult period, Will and I conducted regular meetings, both on a weekly and sometimes daily basis, to ensure that our team was well-informed about the changes taking place. Will and I explained the rationale behind the changes being made and reassured our remaining team members that their jobs and benefits were safe. We reassured them that the corporate restructuring had been successfully completed and that we could now resume our business operations as usual.

This news brought immense relief to our team, with some crying tears of joy, and others showing their gratitude through heartfelt embraces and words of thanks. Witnessing these emotional reactions was both heartwarming and humbling, as it served as a reminder of the significant responsibility we held in our hands; the livelihoods of many individuals depended on our decisions.

We called our corporate restructuring, "growing pains," and as any business that grows rapidly can attest, changes are needed at different phases to help adapt the company to its current reality. We had over-hired, anticipating a growth in our business that did not materialize as quickly as we planned, and as result, we needed to do layoffs and streamline certain tasks to align the expenses with the company's revenues.

Though necessary, implementing change in a company is downright difficult. Laying off people, restructuring departments, outsourcing tasks, pivoting the company's direction, implementing new changes, etc. are all difficult to do because of the human emotions tied to these decisions.

Personally, I found comfort knowing that I was able to endure this difficult moment with my husband and I'm sure he feels the same way. It is during these difficult moments that working with your soulmate once again proves to be highly beneficial. It can be challenging to detach oneself from a significant issue when one is deeply involved in it. Having someone like me, for example, offering a different perspective to consider or offering guidance that is rooted in common interest proves to be invaluable.

Amidst the difficulties we faced at work, we made a deliberate choice to shield our children from the troubles we were encountering. We made a conscious effort to leave work-related issues at the office and focus on creating a nurturing and joyful environment at home. Those moments spent with our kids during our nighttime routine became a cherished escape from the challenges of the day. Their laughter and smiles became a source of joy for Will and me.

The decisions that Will and I made—although hard and heartbreaking—proved to be our saving grace, and we once again bounced back from the deep abyss of financial losses that we faced at the time. Thankfully, we made these decisions just before the global pandemic shook the world the following year.

Chapter Twenty-Four

The COVID-19 Pandemic

William Peña

WHEN WE OVERCOME HARDSHIPS in our lives, we have the mistaken belief that the worst is behind us. We often rationalize that after everything we just went through, life will somehow cut us some slack. Unfortunately, this is not how life works. Sometimes you go from one crisis straight back into another one. There are sometimes no breaks and no moments of rest. This is exactly what happened to us at the beginning of 2020.

During this time, our business was finally turning the corner, and we were back on track to meet our financial targets. January and February of that year were spectacular in terms of financial performance. Then at the end of the first quarter of that year, we began hearing news about a potentially dangerous virus from China that was spreading rapidly within the United States. Every major news outlet was talking about the so-called coronavirus that was spreading rapidly and wreaking havoc in major cities across the world.

Initially, Richelle and I did not take the threat seriously. We figured it was simply the media exaggerating the situation and trying to scare the public. I remember we made derisive comments such as,

"Why is everyone scared of a flu virus? How bad can it be? We haven't had a pandemic in over a hundred years, so why should we worry about this coronavirus causing a global epidemic?" We even attended our daughter Leia's first communion in the middle of March, and I remember the church being full to capacity. We didn't take precautions or pay any attention to the pundits on the news. We felt that all this commotion was transient and we would soon forget about the coronavirus that was supposedly spreading like wildfire.

A few days after Leia's communion celebration, we heard Disney World in Orlando had closed its doors until further notice because several of their guests had become infected with the novel virus. We knew at that point that we were in serious trouble because Disney never closed!

We were all caught off guard because this situation was so unprecedented. There was no resource that we could use to better prepare ourselves. It seemed as though the entire world was learning what to do along the way.

Richelle and I would have daily meetings to discuss the new developments taking place and decipher a response. Since Richelle and I did our administrative work from home, our kitchen counter became the "command center" during the COVID-19 pandemic. There were so many unknowns, so many new developments occurring daily, so much chaos, that it required a careful analysis of the facts and then swift, objective decision-making.

Team members began asking questions about the safety measures that we were implementing to protect them and our patients. Our team was rightfully concerned for their own health and safety. Shortly thereafter, our offices went into a state of complete panic.

We received calls continuously from team members asking us what we were planning to do to address the growing threat from the coronavirus. Were we closing the offices? If not, then when? Were they going to get paid if we closed? Did we have N95 masks and other protective gear readily available? On and on it went for almost two weeks straight.

Finally, Governor Ron DeSantis gave the order that non-essential businesses, including dental offices, needed to cease operations and close in order to preserve masks and other personal protective equipment (PPE), since there was a real, worldwide scarcity of those items.

We finally closed our doors on Friday, March 20, 2020. It was a nerve-racking experience. We were shutting down operations, but we did not know how long we would be closed. So much was going through our minds. *When could we reopen for business? How would we pay for our expenses, such as rent, payroll, etc., if we were not generating any income? How was our team going to support themselves financially during this time?* We were nervous, anxious, and seriously worried about how we were going to survive the pandemic. It was discouraging because we had finally begun making headway in our business just a few months prior. We had made the difficult decisions that ultimately pulled the company from the brink of financial ruin, and now this virus was threatening to put us out of business.

Since we were closed and could not see patients, we generated no income. Our cash reserves would only last us a few months, and there was no mention by the government of when we could resume operations. This was a truly terrifying event.

Despite the uncertainty surrounding the closure of our offices and the financial challenges ahead, we decided to spend quality time as a family rather than give in to constant worry and stress. While the governing authorities worked on a plan to treat this deadly virus, we took advantage of the fact that the kids were home from school to spend quality time as a family. We went on bike rides in our community. We enjoyed our pool and had impromptu barbecues. After the kids were done with homework, we even planned picnics at the park. Richelle and I also worked out together in the mornings and then sat on our patio and enjoyed a steaming cup of coffee.

Our office closure lasted approximately six weeks, and we were finally able to reopen at the beginning of May. Thankfully, the federal government intervened and created the Paycheck Protection Program (PPP) and other loan programs that served as a buoy in the weeks following our reopening.

Little did we know that opening after being shut down for several weeks was going to result in a massive influx of patients to our offices. We were a bit unprepared for this higher than normal surge in patient visits, as the majority of our team members returned to work, but some decided to pursue other work and career opportunities. Since there was a shortage of people looking for job opportunities, it was difficult to rehire some employees, which caused us to be understaffed at the offices. This resulted in prolonged wait times for patients and team members became disgruntled from feeling overworked.

Furthermore, since there was a scarcity of workers and a high demand for them, wages began rising. Shortly after reopening, we received numerous requests from our team members, including the dentists, for a salary increase. While we understood their desire for higher compensation, we had to carefully consider the financial implications of granting these raises. It was evident that approving all the salary increase requests simultaneously would result in significant losses for the company. Richelle and I told them that a salary increase was not possible at the current moment but we would confer with our finance director in a few months to see if there was a possibility at that time. The dentists begrudgingly accepted the wait.

Dental supplies were also in scarce quantities since shipments from other states and countries were delayed, causing these to also dramatically increase in price. This all resulted in an increase in overhead expenses that was threatening to dwindle our capital reserves. Thankfully, we also had a higher than normal demand for our services, at least in the first months after reopening, which helped offset our increase in expenses to a certain extent.

Then chaos once again ensued right before the holidays when the dentists and team members that had demanded a salary increase earlier banded together threatening to leave if we did not grant them the raise that they had previously requested. They told Richelle and me that they were taking a significant risk of becoming infected with COVID-19 while working and that a salary raise was warranted because of it. Besides, they told us, other offices had begun offering more money, and therefore, we needed to follow suit. Richelle and I had checked our finances with our finance director and we honestly could not afford to grant them a raise. We still had financial obligations and loans to pay. We also needed to put money aside in case of another outbreak or government mandated shutdown. There was so much uncertainty in the world during this time that we needed to be prudent with our resources.

Richelle and I made a firm decision not to capitulate to the demands of our team members that had mutinied against us. We recognized that giving in to their requests would establish an unfavorable precedent and would ultimately require us to raise the salaries of all twenty dentists, as well as increase the hourly wages of our dental assistants and front desk personnel. These increases would have inevitably resulted in financial ruin for our business.

We explained this situation to the dentists as clearly as possible, but unfortunately, some of them became upset and chose to leave our company. This left us in a terrible predicament. We now had several vacancies in our business during one of our busiest times of the year—the winter break when kids were off from school. We scrambled to find suitable replacements to no avail. It seemed as though the job market had completely dried up and no one wanted to work.

We were facing another challenging moment and honestly it was starting to feel like a pattern. Whenever our company was performing well and everything seemed to be functioning properly, we would immediately face a serious calamity that threatened to derail us. The swings in our business were abrupt and violent, requiring a lot of courage and resilience to endure them. However, there is only so much your mind and body can endure. Eventually, the pressure becomes insurmountable, pushing you the brink. And that's exactly what happened to me.

Despite the numerous setbacks and challenges we faced during 2020, we had a silver lining. While dealing with a host of issues at our offices, we were presented with an unexpected opportunity to acquire a pediatric dental office. We recognized the potential strategic value of this acquisition and decided to pursue this opportunity despite the numerous uncertainties our company faced. In the next chapter, I'll cover this acquisition in more detail.

Chapter Twenty-Five

God Works in Mysterious Ways

William Peña

T HE OPPORTUNITY TO BUY the dental office that I briefly mentioned has a deeper story. One day in the fall of 2020, I received a random call from an old acquaintance of mine from dental school. He wanted to know if I would be interested in acquiring his dental practice. He told me that he had health issues and wanted to divest his practice so that he could spend more time with his family. He also told me that he lived far from the office and the commute was beginning to wear on him. He wanted us to purchase his office since we had similar practice philosophies. Like us, he also accepted Medicaid and believed in giving back to the community.

I spoke about this potential opportunity with Richelle. She was apprehensive about taking on more loans to buy a practice, especially at a time of so much uncertainty. I argued that unlike our other offices, which were built from scratch and had no patients when we opened them, this practice was already established and was generating a profit. Embracing the possibility of acquiring an existing office, she approached it with an air of skepticism and insisted on personally inspecting the office before committing. Our partnership thrives on our diverse perspectives; we weigh the pros and cons together, making decisions that resonate with both of us. It's in this collaboration that our strength lies.

I made an appointment with the dentist to visit his office. After taking a tour of the facility, Richelle interviewed the team, spoke to the dentist, and did her own inspection of the practice. Although the office was outdated and small, the practice truly shared our same mission and purpose, and it was profitable. After seeing the office and speaking with the staff, Richelle warmed up to the idea of acquiring the practice. She understood that sometimes opportunities present themselves during inopportune times, but life ultimately favors the bold. It was a risk-reward type of scenario. We would be purchasing an office during the midst of a pandemic, but this office could also be a quick add-on to our group and we could achieve our goal of owning eight to ten offices a lot sooner than anticipated. She eventually gave me her blessing to proceed with the acquisition of the office.

During our visit to the practice, the dentist also told us a remarkable story about a life-changing event that occurred while he was at the gym with his friend. At the time, I had no idea this story would affect my life in such a big way.

The dentist told us that one day while working out at the gym, he casually told his friend that he had a family history of cardiac disease. Coincidentally, his friend's father was a renowned cardiologist, and he encouraged the dentist to see him for an evaluation. The dentist was hesitant and told his friend that he felt fine, and that he trained regularly as a triathlete and had never felt chest discomfort or any other heart-related symptom. However, his friend insisted, and the dentist hesitantly went to see the cardiologist for an evaluation. Unbeknownst to the dentist, he had an undiagnosed cardiac defect that required emergency surgery to save his life. He told us that if it wasn't for his friend insisting that he go in for a checkup with his father, he probably would have had an adverse event.

In passing, I told the dentist that I, too, had a family history of cardiac disease. I explained that my maternal grandmother died in her twenties from heart disease and that my mom had a slew of cardiac issues and had experienced two or three ischemic episodes that required hospitalization.

He looked at me inquisitively and asked, "Will, have you gotten your heart checked out by a cardiologist?" I replied that I had not because I felt great and did not have any heart-related issues or symptoms. In fact, I told him, "I run marathons and exercise daily, and I feel fantastic!"

He responded, "I used to run triathlons and never felt a thing, but if it wasn't for my friend's dad, who examined me, I'd probably be dead by now. Go get checked out. Don't mess around with your health, especially when it comes to your heart." I said that I would when I had the time and left it at that.

Honestly, I was not serious about going to a cardiologist for an exam. I was forty years old at the time, and aside from work-related stress and anxiety, I felt perfectly fine.

As negotiations carried forth, he continued pressing me, asking if I had made an appointment with the cardiologist. I kept evading the question, responding with the usual, "I've been busy, but after we get over the sale of your office, I promise you I will."

One day he finally gave me an ultimatum. He told me, "Listen, Will, if you don't make an appointment to see a cardiologist and actually go, I won't sell you my office." I was a tad irritated at his insistence, but seeing that he was adamant, I begrudgingly made an appointment for a cardiac exam.

A few days later, in mid-November, I arrived at my appointment at the cardiologist's office with my son, Adrian. The office was full of older people. Aside from the office staff, we were probably the youngest people there. This only augmented my ire.

After waiting for nearly an hour, I was preparing to leave the office when the nurse called my name. I walked into the examination room with my son, and the nurse gave me a skeptical look and asked, "What is the reason for your visit, Mr. Peña?" I let her know that I was there for an evaluation since I had a family history of heart disease. She took my vitals, and everything seemed to be normal. Then she told me that the doctor would be in shortly and left the room.

When the cardiologist arrived, we exchanged pleasantries, and he proceeded to manually take my blood pressure (BP) with a sphygmomanometer (arguably the most accurate method for taking BP). When he finished taking my BP on my right arm, he simply grunted, "Hmm."

As I work in the healthcare field, I know that when doctors say, "Hmm," it is usually something significant or serious. I asked him, "Doc, is everything okay with my blood pressure?"

He ignored my question and began talking to me about my life and my career—all tactics I knew were meant to help me relax and alleviate the fear-induced "white-coat syndrome" of visiting a doctor's office. After several minutes, he repeated the BP test on my left arm, and after a minute of pause, told me, "Young man, your blood pressure in both arms is elevated. We need to run further tests to evaluate the health of your heart." I was stunned. Prior to that visit, I had never experienced any major illnesses or ailments. I always prided myself on being healthy.

It is amazing how one bit of unwelcome news can pierce your seemingly perfect veil and expose your vulnerability. I had always felt strong, and never once thought that I would have potential health issues in my early forties. At that moment, all I could think of was my kids and Richelle. My children were so little at the time, and they needed their father to be healthy and present in their lives. If something, God-forbid, happened to me, they would be devastated.

When the doctor gave me the status of my cardiac health, I was floored. I had so much to process, but I was in so much shock that I couldn't even think.

Adrian was present in the exam room when the cardiologist informed me of my high blood pressure, and although he did not fully comprehend what had just transpired, he looked worried. He did not ask me anything, but I could tell by the look of his face that he knew something was wrong. At that moment, I felt like a complete fraud and hypocrite. I had made it a point to prioritize my family over my business, but when I was told that I could be diagnosed with hypertension if my blood pressure did not improve, I felt that my priorities had been somehow reversed and my life had become imbalanced.

I also recalled the promise I had made to Richelle when my mother passed away. I told her that I would prioritize my health. I thought that I had kept my word by running and eating better, but I had evidently failed to properly control my stress levels. Worse, instead of scaling back the business, I decided to lean forward and pursue an expansion plan that I thought was feasible, but in hindsight was far too aggressive. This only deepened my feelings of regret.

At that point, I felt trapped and extremely vulnerable. There was no denying that my blood pressure was elevated because of the stress of running our business, but I did not know what the alternatives were. I was in too deep to quit. By this stage, we had established a total of six offices (and were in the process of acquiring our seventh location), and as Richelle had previously cautioned, the managerial challenges were consistently present. I attempted to seek guidance from her, hoping to find comfort in her advice. However, much to my dismay, she, too, was at a loss for words. All I could do at this point was ask God for guidance and wisdom to help me figure out a way forward.

A few weeks later, I underwent the prescribed echocardiogram and stress test to evaluate the function of my heart. The cardiologist interpreted the results of the two tests as normal and told me that he would continue monitoring my blood pressure (which was still elevated but not high enough where I needed antihypertensives). He gave me a three-month follow-up visit, and I was relieved that at least I did not have to take medicine to control my blood pressure. My cardiologist simply recommended lifestyle changes to treat my blood pressure, including stress reduction.

I kept the dentist that was selling his practice to me informed of my visits to the cardiologist. I could not thank him enough for insisting that I do a cardiac exam. He was glad to hear that I was under the supervision of a cardiologist and reiterated what I already knew—I needed to control my stress levels. Feeling uncertain about the future of the business, I made the decision to incorporate meditation into my daily routine. While it provided some relief, it didn't completely alleviate my stress. At that point, it was like placing a band-aid on a gashing wound.

In December of 2020, the dentist and I finally closed on the deal, and I acquired his office. We also worked on a transition plan for him. Honestly, the acquisition was seamless and straightforward. Since his office operated similarly to ours, it was easy to assimilate their operations into our existing infrastructure. Within a few weeks of acquiring the office, the integration was completed.

A few weeks after closing on this deal, I attended Christmas mass with Richelle and the kids. Throughout the day, I experienced a splitting headache that would not subside with over-the-counter analgesics such as acetaminophen or ibuprofen. During mass, the headache became increasingly worse to the point where I could barely concentrate on the celebration. I suspected my blood pressure was high but did not have access to a monitor to measure it.

After mass, we attended a Christmas Eve dinner at Richelle's parents' house. I continued feeling miserable. Finally, I asked my father-in-law for his BP monitor and quickly took my blood pressure. After the machine cycled and turned off, the number on the screen representing my blood pressure startled me: 169/101. A blood pressure like that is dangerously high. It's actually considered a hypertensive crisis. Richelle insisted that I go to the hospital immediately, but it was Christmas Eve and I did not want to ruin the family reunion. Instead I asked my mother-in-law for a bag of ice to place on the crown of my head and two Tylenols to help bring down my headache.

After Christmas, I made an emergency appointment to go see my cardiologist. When I arrived at his office on a Monday afternoon, my BP was a staggering 180/97. I was taken aback at the reading. Aside from the splitting headache that I had during Christmas Eve, I had not experienced any other symptoms. This is why they call hypertension the silent killer.

My cardiologist, too, was shocked. He formally diagnosed me with hypertension. He was concerned that I may experience a stroke or heart attack because of my extremely high blood pressure, and he immediately gave me a prescription for an antihypertensive and diuretic, which I took as soon as the pharmacist dispensed them. He also told me that I needed to relax and take it easy for the next couple of days. Luckily, I had already planned a getaway trip for New Year's with Richelle and the kids.

At that particular moment, however, I felt as though my world came crashing down on me. I had a flashback of my conversation with Richelle a few years earlier when I laid out my grandiose vision of opening "at most" eight to ten offices. I made it seem as though it was a walk in the park. "No big deal," I told myself. I had dismissed the way I was feeling because I did not want to demonstrate weakness as a man and as a provider. I was relentless in honoring my promises to my family and providing for them financially so I had pushed myself to the brink. And now, I was paying the price. I had ignored my own symptoms, my dad's warnings, and I had completely disregarded Richelle's concerns about my stress. I had acted as though I was Superman and I convinced myself that I was infallible. I convinced myself that I could be an amazing father, an outstanding husband, and a great businessman all simultaneously. I could zip from work to an activity or birthday party and it wouldn't affect me. In my mind, this was what responsible men do. They show up and they don't make excuses. It was the indoctrination and the hardwiring that I had gotten from my father during my formative years. I had learned to suppress my emotions and simply get the job done and provide for my family. Now, I was being given the equivalent of a status report of how well my ideology had fared for me and I was devastated.

Chapter Twenty-Six

Dealing With Bad News

Richelle Peña

AFTER WILL WAS DIAGNOSED with hypertension, I was distraught. I guess I never imagined him having a medical condition at such a young age. After the visit to the cardiologist, he came home with Adrian feeling glum. He kissed Leia and Annabelle, and hugged them tight. He then came into the kitchen and asked to talk to me in private to help him clear his mind. The kids were doing homework and dinner was ready, so I went outside to our patio with him.

We sat down, and he lowered his face onto his hand and began to rub his eyes. I asked him if he was okay. He simply responded, "I can't believe this is happening to me."

I told him, "Babe, I know you are worried about your blood pressure, but it's going to be okay. We can get through this. I will help you with whatever you need."

He responded, "The doctor told me that I need to reduce my stress, but there is so much going on at work that I don't know what to do. Two days ago Dr. Vicente put in her letter of resignation. I didn't tell you when it happened because I didn't want to worry you, but I had to drive down to talk with her yesterday after work. She was upset about feeling overworked, and she had an issue with a couple of contractual items, so she decided to resign. I pleaded with her to stay, given the fact that we have worked together for nearly eight years. After much back and forth, she relented and told me that she would think about it. If we lose her, that office will suffer tremendously. Patients love her, and the staff is extremely fond of her."

I told him, "Listen, these are all things that we will eventually see through. I know you are worried about Dr. Vicente and everything else that's happening, but you have to listen to your doctor and look for ways to reduce your anxiety and stress. If all else fails, put your faith in God and let Him fight your battles. We have been in some bad situations before, and God has stepped in to help us. I love you, babe, and I hate seeing you like this."

He thanked me for taking the time to listen to him, and we then went inside to eat dinner as a family, as he didn't want us to stay outside too long because he did not want the kids to get worried. He already felt guilty that Adrian had been present when the cardiologist told him his blood pressure was high and didn't want to worry the girls, too.

During dinner, you would have never known that Will was worried. He seemed jovial, asking the kids how their day went, and per our usual custom during dinner, we asked them if anything positive had occurred throughout the day. We also spoke about our upcoming New Year's trip to Aruba. The kids were excited for this trip, especially since this was the year that the pandemic had caused so many countries to close their borders and would not allow tourists to visit. Aruba was one of the few countries at that time that allowed American tourists to enter, so we planned our escapade to this Caribbean paradise. This was our first international trip of the year, and we were all looking forward to finally relaxing and spending time as a family without worrying about the business.

I hoped this vacation would alleviate some of Will's stress and that he could gain clarity on how to move forward. We cherished traveling not only for the adventure but also as a means to reset our minds, returning to work with a refreshing perspective. During this time, Will appeared to be constantly lost in his own thoughts, burdened by the overwhelming pressures he faced at work, and worried about his health.

Thankfully, Dr. Vicente rescinded her resignation and decided to continue working with us. We expressed our gratitude for her unwavering belief in us and our mission. Will, in particular, felt a sense of relief knowing that his most loyal associate was still by his side, supporting the company. Furthermore, our business was projected to end the year with record breaking revenues and profitability despite all of the problems that we had encountered in 2020. We had also successfully acquired an office and now had a total of seven locations in south Florida. In spite of the positive developments taking place within the company, Will seemed unaffected and unmoved. He still had a lot of introspection to undertake, and I wished for him to discover the answers he sought during our trip.

Throughout our nearly ten years in business together and seventeen years as a couple, I've often found the words to comfort him, guiding him toward the brighter side of things. I've usually been the positive force propelling us through challenging times. However, this time felt different.

Chapter Twenty-Seven

It All Comes Crashing Down

William Peña

A FEW DAYS AFTER my visit to the cardiologist, my family and I boarded a plane to Aruba to spend New Year's. It was going to be a short trip, but I welcomed the break nonetheless. I was dealing with a lot at work and was completely exhausted. I looked forward to relaxing on this Caribbean getaway with my family, and then coming back "recharged" for the new year. As Richelle and I always do when we are away from the office, we take the opportunity to contemplate and envision future plans for ourselves, our family, and our business. Being free of distractions is a great way to practice introspection. My hope on this trip was to seek a fresh perspective and gain insight on the best course of action for the upcoming year.

As I had mentioned earlier, Richelle and I were unsure of how to move forward with our business. I was dealing with high stress levels that were contributing to my hypertension, and my cardiologist had asked for me to relax and find ways to alleviate my stress. However, I found it nearly impossible to do so because we were facing numerous managerial challenges in our business.

Unfortunately, my intentions to engage in a thorough self-reflection were thwarted as soon as we arrived, as I immediately started experiencing dizziness and lethargy. Richelle reassured me that this was a side effect of the heart medicines I was taking. Nevertheless, I felt as though I had no energy. I took it easy, lounging on the beach, and I really enjoyed my time with the kids and Richelle despite feeling terrible. We had amazing dinners, an adventurous excursion through the desert on a four-wheel buggy, and as always, great family conversations. I enjoyed this trip and have fond memories of it.

But on our last night of the trip, I began telling Richelle how sad I was to go back home. I mentioned that I was exhausted, unmotivated, and felt little to no interest in continuing running the business. I had finally reached my breaking point. All those years of suppressing my emotions and being disingenuous with my goals hit me like a pile of bricks.

I looked up at the ceiling and tears began flowing endlessly down my face.

With a concerned look, she told me, "Babe, I'm worried for you. We have dealt with a lot of things in our business in the past and you have gotten worried, but you have never gotten like this before. What's going on? Do you think it's the medicine that's making you feel this way?"

I replied, "I don't know, but I don't think I'm feeling this way because of the medicines I'm taking. I've had time to really slow down and think a lot about you and the kids, and obviously our business, on this trip. I'm scared shitless of something bad happening to me. The pressure of managing our business has really gotten to me and now I have high blood pressure. But I also don't know what to do next. I feel as though I am at an impasse not knowing how to solve my own dilemma. I don't want to continue living stressed and miserable. I have to pretend to our entire team that I have it all figured out, and I have to put a smile on my face even though I am dying inside. I hate telling you this, but I have entirely lost my interest and motivation to continue leading the company."

Richelle was speechless. She was floored by my revelation, and I know that, like me, she also felt stuck and did not know what to do. When we started the company, we obviously didn't know how stressful it would be to manage it. Our original plan for the business morphed many times over the years, but the plan we compromised on and committed to was to grow the business to, what I once believed, was a sustainable organization of up to ten offices. Afterward, I would delegate the operations to a capable manager and we would one day retire. We would then pass our business along to our kids if they wanted it, and if they were not interested in dentistry or business, then we would sell it at that point. But my health really threw a wrench in our plans.

Finally Richelle told me, "Look, let's not make any emotional decisions right now. You have every right to be upset and frustrated, but let's get some sleep and when we get back home, let's continue this conversation."

I knew she was right. I was in an emotional state and in no condition to make life-changing decisions. I figured that perhaps my mood and outlook would improve after getting home and getting back to the grind.

We got home from Aruba on a Saturday. On Sunday, I spent the entire day watching movies at home with the kids. In the evening, we had dinner as a family at one of our favorite local sushi restaurants. I had a great time conversing with the kids and enjoying a glass of wine with Richelle. When we got home in the evening, however, I entered into the same funk as I had the last night in Aruba. Richelle even asked me if I felt depressed. I thought about that for a minute and realized that I was happy being around my family but always sad and anxious on Sunday nights in anticipation of going into work on Monday mornings. It felt eerily similar to how I felt when I worked for my first boss, the same Sunday blues. It was then I came to the realization that I may have what is known as *workplace apathy*.

Once again, though, I didn't know what to do besides go back to work. I went to the office the next day and felt dejected. I was simply going through the motions and felt as though I had completely lost my passion and zeal for my work. That day, I came home, had dinner with the family, and went to bed early. I didn't talk with Richelle about the way I was feeling because there were really no new updates. I continued feeling glum and figured that I was also tired from our recent trip and perhaps from the medicines I was taking.

The next day was just as bad. I wanted nothing more than to hide in my private office at work and not talk with anyone. I even canceled an important meeting I had with my team. I saw my patients in the clinic as quickly as I could and then slipped out of the office and went home. When I got home, I asked Richelle to talk in private with me. We went to our usual spot outside, and I proceeded to tell her exactly how I felt.

"Richelle, I have given it a few days to perhaps bounce back from the way I feel, but honestly, this is beyond feeling burned out. I have lost my entire motivation to lead our team, and I don't think I can continue doing this any longer."

Richelle simply asked, "What do you mean?"

"Well, I have thought about it, and I think we should sell the company. When we got back from our trip, I checked my LinkedIn account and saw messages from two companies that are interested in acquiring our group. I think we should at least meet with them and hear what they have to say. What do you think?"

Richelle appeared shocked. "Whoa, wait a minute! Sell the company? Have you given this enough thought? I thought we wanted to pass our business to our kids one day? What will we do if we sell? Would the amount we get from the sale be enough to sustain our lifestyle? Are you thinking about retiring after a sale, or will you continue working as a pediatric dentist seeing patients? What about me? Where will I work?"

These were all legitimate questions, and I felt selfish for floating such a crazy idea to my wife, who was also my business partner, without having first done my due diligence. I should have done more research and had more concrete answers before proposing the idea of selling the company. I had simply thought about the way I was feeling and didn't stop to think how a decision of this magnitude would affect her. She deserved better.

I apologized and asked her to give me a few days to do my own analysis. I told her that I would research the answers to her questions and then we could make a mutual decision about what the next steps should be regarding our company.

The following day after seeing patients at work, I went into my private office and called a dental practice broker I knew to ask him his opinion on an approximate valuation of our company based on our financial metrics. He asked me a few questions about our business, and after crunching numbers, he gave me a rough estimate of our company's worth. I also asked him logistical questions related to the sale of a company of our size, including how long it would take to sell, my responsibilities post-sale, etc.

Afterward, I did a pro forma analysis of how much money we would net from selling the company. I also calculated how much income I would make working as a pediatric dentist in the clinic seeing patients, and also the cash flow we would receive from leasing our real estate assets back to the buyer.

A day later, I met again with Richelle and presented the analysis I made along with the information given to me by the practice broker. The post-sale plans I proposed to Richelle were as follows: 1) I would continue working as a pediatric dentist seeing patients in the clinic, earning a salary for my clinical duties; 2) We would collect rent from our real estate assets that we were leasing to the new company; and 3) Richelle would have some time after a potential sale to figure out her next career move.

Richelle was satisfied with the information I presented to her because the income we would receive according to my proposal would be on par with what we were making at the time. We would also make enough money from the sale of the business to buy our dream home, put some into our personal savings and our kid's college fund, and invest a portion of the proceeds into real estate to generate passive income.

I was excited to hear that Richelle was onboard with the idea of possibly selling the company. There were a lot of unknowns left, but knowing that my wife stood beside me and supported me through this life-changing decision was extremely gratifying for me. Moreover, the idea of selling our business and handing off the managerial responsibilities to a capable operator really appealed to me. We had a successful business and it deserved to be led by someone with more experience and with the proper resources to continue growing it. I would also have more time post-sale to be fully present with my kids, attend their events, and not be stretched for time as I once had been. It was a win-win scenario and I was once again excited about the future possibilities.

Chapter Twenty-Eight

The Light at the End of the Tunnel

Richelle Peña

A s WILL MENTIONED IN his previous chapters, 2020 was a crazy year for us as a married couple and as business partners. We dealt with countless issues related to the pandemic such as our offices closing for several weeks, inflationary pressures, and team members resigning because we were unable to give them a raise.

Will and I were also dealing with a myriad of issues at home as well, and I'd like to give you that part of the picture. The kids' school was closed, and all learning took place online via videoconferencing from home. As many parents can attest, we had to become educators virtually overnight. Leia, for example, was taking science and had numerous questions on the subject matter that neither Will nor I could help her with. Even though Will and I were both science majors in college, we had forgotten most of the concepts. Besides, who really remembers the function of each part of a cell or can explain the Krebs cycle to an eight-year-old?

Her grades began falling, which is atypical for her since she has always been an A-student. Adrian was also struggling with math. This was frustrating for both Will and me, and we had to look for tutors (online, of course) who could help them with their classes. Luckily, Annabelle was not affected as much because she was in kindergarten during the school closures that took place during the pandemic.

The kids were also bored with being home all day. Fortunately, we heard about a group class that was training kids for a triathlon event and learned that all the classes took place outdoors (which was perfect during COVID). Despite all the issues we were both dealing with at work and the stress we felt, we went with our kids to the park so that they could get out of the house and socialize with their friends from school who were also participating in the classes. Being out in the fresh air was also beneficial for Will and me. It was great getting out of the office or out of the house and being in an outdoor setting with our kiddos.

2020 was also a year that changed our professional lives. As Will had mentioned, we wanted our business to be a legacy for our children. We never considered selling our business as an option, not even during the most difficult moments of our company's history. Will's health and his burnout changed all of that for us.

When he proposed the idea of selling our company to me, I was extremely nervous since I did not know what our life would be like post-sale. Of course, I asked him a barrage of questions related to how the process worked, proceeds from the sale, etc., and when he was unable to answer them, he really made me edgy.

To be frank, I initially did not want to sell our business when Will proposed the idea to me. Although I was stressed dealing with the kids, managing the call center, and leading the business with Will, I chose not to complain. Perhaps it was my upbringing that taught me never to protest when faced with a challenging situation. I learned from my parents that the best way to deal with problems is to find creative solutions to resolve them. This is something I always did throughout my professional career, starting when I began working at the pharmacy. If there is an issue at work, or even at home with our kids, my mind goes into overdrive trying to find a solution.

However, that all changed after our New Year's trip to Aruba. Seeing Will stressed, aggravated, and feeling burned out, really made me stop and realize that his health was in jeopardy. He had been diagnosed with hypertension prior to our trip, and I feared losing my husband at an early age because of the immense stress and pressure he felt while running our company. I was really concerned for his health, and knew that we needed to pivot from our original plan of owning our company in perpetuity, but I also needed to know how we would provide financially for our family.

Once Will showed me his analysis, however, I fully supported the initiative of putting our business on the market for an eventual sale. I was no longer going to let him pursue wealth at the expense of his own health. The kids and I needed Will to be healthy and a part of our lives for a very long time. Although I was scared, I realized that the fear came from my mind, warning me of the many unknowns that lay ahead.

A few days after we agreed to explore a possible sale, Will made appointments with the CEOs of the two companies that had reached out to him via LinkedIn. We met with each CEO for lunch in mid-January of 2021. We kept the meetings casual and asked them general questions such as, "What attracted you to our company?" "What added benefits can you bring to our company and team?" "What are your plans for our company if we decide to sell?" and "How does the acquisition process work?"

Both gentlemen were very cordial during lunch. We also gave them a tour of our facilities, and they were genuinely impressed with our offices and team members. We engaged the services of the practice broker that Will was acquainted with and began the long process of putting our beloved company up for sale.

To be honest, we actually never listed our business for sale. We decided that the two contending companies could be viable owners of our business and allowed them to bid for our company. Each company made us an offer that was attractive to both of us. We deliberated on the matter for several days, reviewing the positives and negatives of each company. Eventually, we decided to explore an opportunity with one company over the other. We liked this particular company because they were specialists in our field—pediatric dentistry—and also because they had a "team first" mentality, accepted Medicaid, and saw patients with special needs at their offices. We both felt as though it was a match made in heaven.

Before making such a life-altering decision, however, it was important for Will and me to fly up to their headquarters and see some of their other offices and meet the other members of their management team. We flew up to their administrative offices, met their entire leadership team, and visited several of their pediatric dental offices. We not only witnessed their operations in person, but we also got the opportunity to speak with the office managers and several staff members, and we got a good feel of their team culture. Will and I agreed that the team members we spoke to seemed jubilant, and the atmosphere at the offices was upbeat and positive.

After our tour of the offices, we went out to dinner with the leadership team to acquaint ourselves with the individuals that potentially would manage our company. In my opinion, going out to dinner with someone is the best way to see how they truly are, deep inside.

The manner in which they treat the service workers, for example, gives you a good gauge of how they treat others. If they are rude or condescending, and have no manners, then it is a good indication of how they will treat their own team.

I liked the idea of going out to dinner with their team because it was a more casual environment compared to the boardroom where we met initially to discuss business matters. Will and I observed the manner in which they treated the staff at the restaurant and how they were amicable to everyone at dinner. This was a positive sign for us.

Thankfully, all the members of the leadership team that we dined with were exactly the type of people that we were looking for to take over our business. They were all down-to-earth, friendly, and professional. Seeing their operations in action and meeting the leadership team really affirmed our decision to sell our company to this group. We got back to Florida, and a few days later, we signed a letter of intent (LOI).

I felt a sense of contentment and a strong conviction that we were making the correct choice. However, a thought began to linger in my mind—what would it be like to no longer work alongside my husband after the sale? Since our time together in graduate school at Nova Southeastern University, Will and I had always been inseparable. Every accomplishment we achieved was a result of our teamwork. The idea of not working with him was something that I couldn't help but ponder. Not working with Will was something I would have to get used to and I hoped that perhaps in the future we could join forces on another venture. For now, though, we had to move forward with the sale of our business.

We celebrated the milestone of signing the agreement with our kids. Although they were young at the time (Adrian was nine years old, Leia was eight years old, and Annabelle was six years old), they understood that this was a major accomplishment for us as a family. That night, Will and I toasted with champagne and shared our dream of moving into our favorite community with the kids. They were excited by the prospect of living in a bigger house in an exclusive neighborhood. We also spoke about the trips that we would take in the following years, and they beamed with exuberance at our future plans for our family. As a parent, it's in these moments you realize that all the hard work and sacrifices you make are really to make your family happy and secure.

After all that he went through during the tenure of our business and after being miserable for so long, Will finally gleamed with happiness. He was finally seeing the light at the end of the tunnel. As his partner, I was happy for him and proud of all our accomplishments in our life up to that point.

This moment of happiness, however, would be short-lived. Little did we know how hard the next few months were going to be as we navigated the sale of our business.

Chapter Twenty-Nine

Trouble in Paradise

William Peña

D URING THE SALE OF a business, after signing the letter of intent, a process called "quality of earnings," or QE, begins. This process was conducted by a third-party accounting firm hired by the acquiring company to audit and scrutinize our financials and all pertinent documents in the company. Since we had so many business entities, all with separate financials, these documents needed to be thoroughly reviewed. In my opinion, aside from going through dental school, undergoing the QE has been one of the most rigorous and stressful periods of my entire life—not because of any fault of the acquiring company, or even the firm conducting the QE, but because of my situation with the finance director of our company at the time.

Our finance director, who was in charge of our company's bookkeeping and our corporate finances, called me one day and told me that, sadly, he had been diagnosed with a serious health condition. His condition was so dire that he needed to move to another city immediately in order to receive specialized treatment.

He could barely work, given his delicate health condition, and understandably, he fell behind on his tasks. The company's finances were in complete disarray.

This unfortunately occurred at a time when his contribution was needed the most, since the sale of the business hinged on our company being able to provide accurate financials to the acquiring firm. Since he was unable to work most of the time, the valuation process became hindered and was delayed on several occasions. To make matters worse, he was the only person in the company who understood our corporate money flows and could provide financial statements—a colossal design error on our part. No one else could provide or decipher our company's financials.

At one point, we thought we would never close on our deal. A closing seemed so close at one point, but like a mirage, it got further and further away as we approached it. It seemed as though the harder we all worked to make it a reality, the more elusive it became. I was tired from all the back-and-forth, from the extensive due diligence, and I was also seriously concerned about the health of my finance director, especially since he had a young family.

The stress of the deal really got to me. I knew that I was on the verge of a mental breakdown because I was stressed and irritable, even at home. I began experiencing heart palpitations. I have always been good about compartmentalizing my emotions and doing my best to keep my work and home life separate. But during the spring of 2021, I was at my wits' end, and my kids began noticing my foul mood. They would ask Richelle, "What's wrong with Daddy? Is he okay? Why is he always upset?" I did my best to be more chipper to no avail. There were so many unknowns swirling in my head, and at the forefront was trying to get this deal to actually close.

The broker that I hired to assist us had tried to mentally prepare me for the Herculean effort involved in the sale of a business of our size, but I underestimated the amount of work that it would entail. I had prided myself on having everything properly organized, but despite other facets of the business being in order, our financial statements remained unfinished, and the acquiring company could not complete the evaluation. Every time my finance director would submit the financials, more questions would arise. By this point, I was ready to pull the plug and get out of the deal. I had reached my breaking point and could not take the immense pressure I was going through.

Thankfully, I had the unwavering support of Richelle and my father, who came to my rescue and helped alleviate my stress. Richelle has always been a beacon of positivity and a breath of fresh air in my life. No matter how dire the situation seems, she always manages to find the silver lining.

Similarly, spending time with my dad and listening to music with him became a source of relaxation and comfort. He has always been there to lend an empathetic ear, allowing me to vent my frustrations, and then providing a healthy dose of reality. His ability to put things into perspective is truly a gift. No matter how overwhelming an issue appears, my dad always shows me that it can be managed with ease.

I was fortunate to have my family by my side as they helped me get through this incredibly stressful period. I also prayed a lot during this time. I had done all I could do and I put the rest in God's hands. It was comforting knowing that despite the whirlwind of problems and issues swirling all around me, He was there to offer me solace.

Five months after signing the LOI, and in the midst of the grueling quality of earnings process, we traveled to Hawaii for a family vacation to celebrate my son's tenth birthday. One day while in Maui, I received a call from my broker that really put me over the top. He told me that the company was considering revising their initial offer because the financials that we originally submitted seemed inaccurate. I was floored. I had done an entire projection of what we would do with the sale proceeds, and now this was going to potentially affect our post-sale plans.

I immediately felt a rush of frustration because I couldn't untangle nor interpret the mess of our company's financials that were caused by our finance director. I was angry at myself for allowing our finance director to have full autonomy over our company's finances. Richelle and I had given him free rein, and little oversight, to organize the company's finances in a manner considered to be the best for our business. This was our error, and now we were in the predicament where our company could potentially get valued at a way lesser amount than what we were originally told, namely because we failed to have checks and balances within our own financial department.

Richelle and I were obviously anguished by this bit of unwelcome news from our broker. My mind started racing, *Would our post-sale plans be affected? Would it still make financial sense to sell the company at this new lower valuation? What were Richelle and my kids going to think of me since I had sold them on the idea of financial independence post-sale and this single call had the potential to derail our plans?*

Since it was my son's birthday celebration, we went on a snorkeling expedition off the coast of Maui. I did not want our issues from work to affect our trip, so I tried my best to enjoy the moment. My mind, however, kept ruminating on the conversation I had a few hours earlier with my broker, and it was causing me a great deal of trepidation.

When we all got back to our Jeep Wrangler after the snorkeling excursion to drive back to our hotel, I told Richelle, "I am worried about our deal. Do you think it'll go through? What if they give us a valuation so low that we are unable to sell?" She quipped, "I'm worried too, but we can't keep going in circles about what may or may not happen. We are obsessing about our situation based on hypotheticals. Why don't you call the broker and the finance director and see what the issue is and how we can fix it?"

I did not want to ruin the day with the quandary we were having with our business sale, but I knew that if I did not get concrete answers about where the deal was headed, I would not be able to relax for the remainder of the week that we stayed in Hawaii, and this might affect the time Richelle and the kids had.

Following Richelle's advice, I picked up my phone and saw that I had no reception. I drove a mile or so down the road and still had none. I drove another mile, checked the phone and still nothing. This only further fueled my anxiety. Finally, on the crest of a mountain pass, I got a few bars of reception. I immediately parked our Jeep on the side of a steep cliff and called my broker and finance director, and also a few members of the acquiring company. It was a pretty intense and heated conversation. Even worse, my children were present during my conversation and felt both curious and nervous about what was going on.

On the call, Richelle and I were reassured that the deal would go through and that although the deal seemed to have reached a stalemate, we were actually inching along. No mention was made, however, on the final valuation of our company, since the finance director still needed to make a few edits to the company's financials.

At one point during the conference call, I muted the phone and asked Richelle for her thoughts on how to proceed. A part of me really wanted to pull out of the deal because it was causing me so much internal strife.

She told me, "Will, if we cancel this deal, we will be back to square one. We have to remember the reasons *why* we are doing this. Your health is being affected by continuing to run the company, and you are miserable managing it. I want this deal to finally go through, even if they give us a lower valuation for our company. You are unhappy, and without knowing it, you are causing a lot of tension within our family. I don't like seeing you like this. I know you are worried and have a lot of 'what-ifs' regarding the outcome of this deal, but I have a feeling that it will all work out in the end."

Richelle was absolutely right. I knew that I was being myopic because I wanted my pain to stop. I was tired of the sleepless nights, the constant worrying, and my mind constantly racing. Furthermore, I was worried about my heart condition, but knew that I was "protected" because of the medicines I was taking. Nevertheless, I was worried that I may experience worsening cardiac symptoms because of the constant tension related to this deal. My negative aura was also contaminating my household, and I knew that it was not good for Richelle or the kids to see me like this. Despite my hesitation, I agreed to proceed.

A few days after arriving from Hawaii, my finance director notified us that the financials were finally ready. He submitted these to the broker and the acquiring company. I still wondered if our valuation was going to be affected based on the revised financials, but I remained optimistic.

A week or so later, I received a call from our broker, and he gave us really bad news. Based on the revised financials submitted by our finance director, our company was worth substantially less. I'm not talking a thousand or even hundreds of thousands less, but a few million dollars less than the original valuation! I was incensed and yelled at my broker, but I realized shortly after that it was misplaced anger. This was not his fault.

Our broker told me that he had reviewed the revised financials submitted by our finance director and the numbers he had submitted made sense; the acquiring company thought the same. Although his explanation of the numbers made sense, I was so devastated by the news that I simply hung up the phone. Shortly after speaking with him, I received the revised, albeit lower offer for our business.

As I always do when faced with bad news, I pray for God's guidance first, and then I seek out my other source of wisdom and enlightenment—Richelle. We discussed what I had just learned from the broker and we reviewed the new offer. She made me realize that although the offer was a few million dollars less than the original bid, it was still a great valuation of our company, and we could still achieve the financial goals that we had planned for with some minor modifications. We were still able to buy our dream home and our beach investment property, and I was still able to continue working in the clinic. Thankfully, our revised valuation changed none of our primary objectives.

We decided to move forward with the deal. The quality of earnings process was officially over, our valuation was solidified, and we now headed toward the fun stuff—contractual agreements.

Reviewing the revised offer for our company as a family. We ultimately decided to accept the new valuation. It was time to move on to the next chapter in our lives.

By the time we had to review the legion of agreements involved with the sale of our company, I was so spent from the arduous quality of earnings process, that dealing with the legal stuff seemed a breeze by comparison. Don't get me wrong, it was still stressful, and there were many items that needed to be negotiated, but it paled in comparison to the nerve-racking process of undergoing a quality of earnings.

Slowly, I felt the pressure and tension easing up a bit. I could, once again, finally see the light at the end of the tunnel. We were inching along this deal and the most grueling part of it was finally behind us. My mood slowly transitioned from being morose, to now feeling optimistic and cheerful. Now that we had a final, concrete valuation for our business (and we knew how much we would net from the sale after paying off our debts), I once again sat around the dinner table and spoke about our future plans with Richelle and the kids. We even coordinated an elaborate dinner—just the five of us—at a high-end restaurant in Miami on the Friday right before the closing date to celebrate the culmination of our life's work up to that point.

Several weeks before the closing of our business sale scheduled for mid-August of 2021, Richelle and I had to break the news to our team that we were being acquired. We had told key members of our administrative team that a sale of the company was being pursued, but we unfortunately had to omit the news from the rest of our company's team members.

Although we wanted to be transparent and straightforward with our team (since this is part of our culture), we also knew that a hint of suspicion that we were selling the company would set off possible panic and a mass exodus of personnel from our offices. We know that people, in general, are hesitant to embrace change, especially those that may have significant ramifications to them personally. There would be questions from our team members such as, "Will our business culture change?" "Will my salary be reduced?" "Will they still honor my paid time off?" "What if the new management considers my position redundant or obsolete? Will I lose my job?" If they were to ask Richele and me these questions during the contract negotiations, we would not know what to say.

After we were done drafting the legal agreements and knew for certain that we were going to close on our deal, a team from the acquiring company came down to Florida and briefed us on how to relay the news of the acquisition to the rest of our team and how to answer their multitude of questions. Afterward, we arranged a meeting with our entire team. Richelle and I thought that the most efficient way to relay the news to everyone in the company, simultaneously, was by hosting a town-hall-style meeting via videoconferencing.

On the call, we thanked everyone for their service and loyalty to the company. Richelle and I reminded them of our core values and guiding principles, and I personally explained that I had lost my enthusiasm in leading the company. Then, finally, we told them that we were being acquired by an organization who resembled a much larger version of our own company. We explained the alignment in vision between the new organization and ourselves, emphasizing our commitment to serving the dental needs of the community. Richelle and I also took turns explaining the benefits of being acquired by a larger company, namely, more growth opportunities, better salary (everyone would receive an automatic small raise upon the deal closing), retirement savings through a company-sponsored 401(k), and comprehensive health benefits (including vision and dental). We also answered a few questions from staff members and did our best to allay their fears with this transition. Everyone seemed to take the news extremely well. In fact, no one left the company after we closed on the deal a few weeks later.

Approximately two weeks after our important vis-à-vis with the staff, we would finalize the sale of our company. Richelle and I were both ecstatic that we were finally closing this amazing, yet stressful chapter in our lives. Creating, growing, and then selling our company was our most significant professional accomplishment up to that point, and we were proud of the work we had done. We had swam against the current and done something that many people thought to be hard or outrageous. I will be honest. It was incredibly difficult. It has been one of the most arduous endeavors I have personally undertaken. There were too many difficult conversations that needed to be had, too many life-altering decisions that needed to be made, too many rollercoaster types of emotions, and too many frightening moments. Although I consider myself to have a high tolerance for risk, there were times when I felt that I had gone too far (like the time we tripled the size of our company in one year and then doubled again two years later).

I had always lived by the mantra, "No pain, no gain," in pretty much everything I do, and I applied this same principle to growing our business. I felt that I needed to take a magnified risk to grow the company, and despite the inherent pressures of running it, I dismissed how that pressure would affect me, or worse, my family. Fortunately, God put up proper warning signs that were hard to miss—my elevated heart pressure, the insomnia, the constant worrying that eventually led to acute anxiety—which made me reconsider my life's goals. I know in hindsight that if I would have continued dismissing those divine signals and continued being disingenuous about the way I was feeling, I have little doubt in my mind that I would have suffered a life-threatening event.

After putting aside my pride, my ego, and being truly honest with myself did I realize that I did not need to build a sprawling enterprise to feel successful. I realized after doing the analysis prior to putting the company up for sale, that I don't need billions, or even millions, to make me happy and feel accomplished. With our deal, we could achieve all our financial goals, and live a peaceful and purposeful life.

The notion of establishing a nationwide company as a means to achieve success and fulfillment was simply a figment of my imagination that I had nurtured since my youth. It consumed my thoughts and preoccupied my mind for the better part of my existence. I had created an image of what I envisioned success to be and held on to that image regardless of the realities I faced. Anything short of accomplishing nationwide domination was failure in my eyes. By God's grace, I had the foresight to come to my senses and learned to see my life differently.

Success was not defined by what I could accomplish solely with the business. Success, as I learned to define it, was achieving financial freedom while remaining true to one's values, being a present and loving father, and a doting and supportive husband.

I understood at that moment that all the pain and suffering I had endured while operating our business had a higher purpose. As famed Navy Seal and endurance athlete, David Goggins, famously stated, "Pain unlocks a secret in the mind, one that leads to both peak performance and beautiful silence." It was God's way of helping me see life differently. It was so that I could learn to keep the balance and to be less idealistic. It was to understand what is truly important in this ephemeral life of ours—to cherish the moments we have with our loved ones, to utilize our heavenly gifts to help those less fortunate, and to live a life of gratitude and service.

I am truly grateful for the hardships and grueling moments of building our business. It transformed me in ways I couldn't imagine. Learning to let go of my fallacious vision for my life was a liberating experience. I could now focus on creating a better future with my family. I was young, after all, when we sold the business (I was forty-one years of age when we closed on the sale) and I had an entire life where I could continue doing something meaningful. Hopefully, I could do it together with Richelle.

Chapter Thirty

A Day to Always Remember

Richelle Peña

O N August 16, 2021, we finally closed on our long-awaited deal and were officially a part of a larger dental organization. It took us close to eight months to finally close on this deal after arriving from our New Year's trip to Aruba and deciding to sell the company.

It was crazy to think that our roller-coaster ride of opening and managing our business had finally come to an end. Yet, we were optimistic about the possibilities that this sale would bring us. About a month after the sale of our business, we would be closing on the purchase of our dream home and an investment property in an exclusive beach town on the west coast of Florida known as Captiva. We were beginning a new chapter in our lives, and we were thrilled. Most importantly, we were no longer going to have the immense pressure of managing our business moving forward. Granted, there would be a transition period of approximately four to six months, but at least a new management team would be taking over our business.

I was taking time off to rest, mentally recover, and reconsider my own life's plans. Building our company was exhausting for me, and I realize in hindsight, that I, too, was constantly worrying, not only about our company's survivability, but also about Will's health. I maintain composure in spite of tension or strenuous circumstances, but reflecting on this period now, I realize that our entrepreneurial trek had taken its toll on me.

Don't get me wrong, I love working with my husband. As he mentions, our relationship is synergistic. We complement each other's personalities and bring out the best in one another. I may be serene and positive, but I am not inherently a risk-taker. I may often fall victim to analysis paralysis, unable to make decisive decisions for fear of repercussions, or simply getting it wrong and feeling embarrassed. Will, on the other hand, *is* a risk-taker, so we balance each other.

We created an incredible company with a magnanimous mission because we leveraged each other's skill sets and then supported one another on an emotional level. As he mentions many times throughout the book, I was the calm he needed when he faced a multitude of challenges managing the operations of the business. In turn, when I was apprehensive of making a decision—quitting my job as a pharmacist and joining his startup dental business back in 2011 or when we acquired the dental office during the pandemic, for example—he would put me at ease by explaining the reasons why the decision made sense.

During our tenure operating our business, I also gleaned valuable lessons from Will's business acumen and his ability to lead and inspire our team. As a result, I evolved into a more accomplished businesswoman than I could have ever become working in a corporate environment or at the pharmacy.

After doing my part to transition the business to the acquiring firm, I wanted to take a break from work so that I could fully immerse myself into motherhood. Although I am eternally grateful for the flexible schedule I had for many years that allowed me to spend quality time with Adrian, Leia, and Annabelle, I now wanted to spend more time volunteering at their school and plan fundraising activities for our church. This was my moment to do something that I found meaningful and in accordance with my own principles, and am thankful that I was able to do it.

The day of the closing was amusing. As part of our deal to sell the company, Will wanted to continue working as a pediatric dentist seeing patients in the clinic. On the day of closing, he was scheduled to work and, not being one to miss a workday under any circumstance, he decided to close on the deal remotely from his private office during his lunch break. I joined him during lunch, did the closing, and later left to pick up the kids from school. It was surreal to think that we had just achieved one of our greatest milestones—we had sold the company for a large sum and had achieved financial independence—and it was still business as usual for both Will and me. We honestly did not process the weight of what had just occurred. The fact that we had just sold the company had not hit us. It was not until we all got home that the weight of our decision truly impacted us.

Over a celebratory glass of California pinot noir at our favorite Indian restaurant in Fort Lauderdale, Will and I began reminiscing on our journey over the past decade. We had embarked on what many thought was a utopian mission. We were starting a mission-based company, with an altruistic purpose in the middle of one of the worst economic recessions since the Great Depression. We had a rough start, but managed our business to financial success through a host of challenges along the way. Then, in the latter end of our journey, we faced the COVID-19 pandemic, which was not only unprecedented, but presented its unique challenges for us as well. Despite the staggering odds, we thrived as a company and then later successfully sold the company to a viable organization.

We then later called our parents to share the good news that we had finally closed on our deal. They were ecstatic when they heard the news. As immigrants that came to this country in search of a better life, they were obviously proud to see that their son and daughter were experiencing so much joy and success. It is the dream of every immigrant parent that leaves their native country to see their children succeed and to know that their sacrifices were worth all the pain and struggles that they endured. And Will and I always knew that we wanted to pay homage to our mom and dad, whom we personally witnessed sacrifice so much to provide us and our siblings with a better life.

For us, our success is their success.

After the sale was finalized and all the paperwork was signed, we made the collective decision to go on a family trip to Sarasota in order to commemorate this significant milestone. The burden that had been weighing us down was finally lifted, and we eagerly anticipated the opportunity to spend quality time together as a family. The first half of the year had been consumed by anxiety and apprehension, so we were truly looking forward to cherishing these moments and fully embracing the present. Gone were the days of dreading phone calls and being preoccupied with pressing matters. We could now fully immerse ourselves in the present moment, free from any worries or concerns.

On this trip, we had long family talks and discussed the events that were taking place in the next several weeks. We talked about the memories we would create together at our new home, our visits to the beach house, etc. It was a great moment as a family, not only because we were celebrating our incredible achievement, but because both Will and I finally felt happy and optimistic about our future.

Some time after moving into our dream home, I read Kevin Hart's memoir, *I Can't Make This Up: Life Lessons,* and I ran across a line in his book that really resonated with me, "It is through our most extreme experiences that the biggest growth happens—if we survive them." After reading this line, I reflected on our own journey and smiled. I knew that the struggles we endured had added tremendous value to us as parents, soulmates, and entrepreneurs. We had grown in many facets of our life—in our faith, our love and respect for one another, and our approach to parenthood. I knew that by going through this together, we had learned so much from one another, and Will and I were able to connect on a deeper level. Life really tested our core values and knowing that we stayed faithful and disciplined to them, despite the numerous calamitous situations we faced, was awe-inspiring.

A few months after the high of the business sale wore off and the dust settled, I began thinking, *What's next?* For the most part, our identity and purpose had been tied to the business, and now that all that was in the hands of a new owner, Will and I struggled to find meaning in our professional lives. The experience of being a business leader brought me immense satisfaction and fulfillment. I relished the intellectual challenge of tackling intricate problems and found great joy in the art of mentoring individuals to become exceptional leaders. After the sale, there were no more challenges or fires to put out. The sudden lack of meetings and the absence of requests for my input was a stark contrast to the fast-paced environment I had grown accustomed to. It was the quintessential definition of a paradox. The decision to sell our business was primarily driven by the overwhelming stress and pressure that accompanied the managerial responsibilities. However, little did I anticipate the sense of boredom and aimlessness that would ensue once those responsibilities were relinquished. In the lead-up to the sale, I had envisioned a life free from the burdens of work, where I could devote my time to personal pursuits and endeavors. Yet, I soon realized that my expectations were completely misguided.

Will also approached me and told me that he, too, was struggling to find true purpose in his professional life. He told me that all the free time he now had was driving him crazy, and he felt unproductive. In his words, he told me that he felt "intellectually unstimulated" and wanted to do something else besides work in the clinic, but he had not found anything meaningful to pursue.

We found ourselves at a crossroads once again, unsure of which path to take. We brainstormed various possibilities, such as venturing into the world of online business, establishing a real estate company, or even pursuing a career in teaching. However, none of these options ignited the same level of passion and excitement that had initially inspired us to create our company, American Pediatric Dental Group.

While we found our next career path, we made a conscious decision to embrace our newfound freedom and rejuvenate our minds and spirits. These introspective discussions, however, became a recurring theme in our lives, spanning a period of approximately two years.

During this lull, we seized the opportunity to remodel our new home. My days were filled with meetings with contractors and designers, as we meticulously planned and executed each aspect of the renovation. Simultaneously, we fully embraced the joys of parenthood, dedicating ourselves wholeheartedly to our children and their endless number of after-school activities. We enjoyed the precious moments spent together as a family, cherishing the opportunity to be fully present in their lives. Amidst the chaos of home renovations and the demands of parenting, we also found ourselves contemplating our next professional endeavor.

Finally in the summer of 2023, we had an epiphany. Why not use our knowledge and expertise gained by managing our business, raising a family, and nurturing our marriage to help other entrepreneurs achieve their own goals and dreams? To take it a step further, why not teach business owners not only how to achieve financial success, but also teach these same entrepreneurs to be better parents and better spouses or life partners? We figured that there are probably other business owners that are stressed, anxious, and burned out, just like we once were. We could help them navigate those turbulent waters and achieve financial freedom so they, too, could pursue other interests outside of work.

In addition, Will and I came to the realization that this type of work not only aided other entrepreneurs in achieving their professional and personal goals, but it would also be intellectually stimulating for us. Each business owner has unique requirements and challenges that they may be facing. Based on these needs, we could develop a tailored plan to assist them in addressing their concerns. With our business experience and expertise in resolving organizational issues, we were in an ideal position to support our colleagues. Furthermore, as a significant part of our responsibilities involved creating videos and delivering on-air presentations, I would also fulfill my aspiration of becoming a media personality—a desire that I had been secretly harboring since childhood.

It was like a light bulb had gone off.

Our goal to become business consultants really piqued our interests and fueled our passion. It kindled the same fire within us as when we began our pediatric dental business over a decade ago. We had found a purpose, and it was time to make that dream into a reality.

The first thing we did was to give others a glimpse into our lives. Through our social media platforms, we showed others how we carefully balanced our many work and parental responsibilities. For example, we posted videos of our fitness routines, pictures and videos of our family on vacation, and business tips and advice.

I also hired a public-relations specialist, who has helped me land television and podcast opportunities so that I can speak about family and business. I now have the opportunity to both do something that I have wanted to do since I was young, and use these forums to speak on subjects that are important to Will and me and our new consulting business.

We still have a long journey ahead of us, but I'm glad we took the first step. The true outcome of our latest venture will be revealed in due time. But for now, we are putting tremendous efforts into our new business and are driven by our newfound mission. Despite the hurdles and difficulties that lie ahead on our uncharted path, we can at least find comfort in the fact that we have each other for support. It is reassuring to know that we are venturing beyond our comfort zone as a united and formidable duo, rather than facing the challenges alone. Knowing this is extremely comforting.

I hope that our story has inspired you to reflect on your own journey. Perhaps our story kindles a desire to take the entrepreneurial leap. However, before taking the plunge, I urge you to peruse the epilogue. In this section, I delve into additional insights and considerations. Furthermore, I will share our tried-and-true tips and strategies, enabling you to form your own conclusions on whether you and your partner can also attain triumph in constructing a prosperous business together and become your own rendition of a "power couple."

Traveling has always been a part of our family. This was our summer trip to Santorini after the sale of our business.

Epilogue

Our Tips to Success

Richelle Peña

WILL AND I HAVE had an incredible journey together. We successfully managed a multimillion-dollar, multi-location organization while also prioritizing our time with our three children and nurturing our marriage. What was the secret to our success? It all began with the fundamental elements of trust, respect, and faith, which enabled us to function as a cohesive team, excelling in both our professional and personal lives.

From our experiences of navigating the roller coaster ride of business while raising a family, we learned many things. The first is that working with your spouse can be the greatest thing that's ever happened to you, or it can be extremely detrimental to your marriage. The outcome, of course, is highly dependent on how well you ascertain compatibility *prior* to embarking on a business journey with your significant other. As Will mentioned in the preface, understanding your personal dynamic beforehand is crucial to your success as business owners and as a married couple.

Secondly, entrepreneurs should not take a magnified risk with their business as we did. This will only lead to unnecessary stress and tension in your marriage, as you have personally witnessed when we shared our story of opening our first office at the beginning of this book. We believed strongly in our company's vision and mission, but did we have to go all-in as we did in the beginning? Absolutely not! Accepting Medicaid and building a large office around this concept was a gamble. Reimbursements are low and the compliance requisites are high, and many dentists are apprehensive of accepting it for these reasons. Back then, the only places children and families could turn to if they had Medicaid was dental schools and community centers. Therefore, we took a huge risk by investing all our money and taking out huge loans to build a business around an unproven concept. The gamble obviously paid off handsomely for us, but we don't suggest others taking this type of outlandish risk. Start small, prove your concept, then build big afterward.

Furthermore, follow a holistic and balanced approach to work and your personal life. This has been a central theme in our book. Although managing our company was time-consuming and over-whelming, we made time for the things that mattered *most* to us—our family, our health, and our friends. One effective approach to achieving a balance between work and your personal life is to establish a clear hierarchy of priorities, much like we did when we developed our *G.F.B Principle*. What are the three or four most significant goals or priorities you wish to achieve in your life? List them out in sequential order and then commit to honoring those priorities. If you find yourself becoming unbalanced and experiencing a shift in priorities (similar to what happened to us on numerous occasions), there's no need to engage in self-flagellation. Instead, acknowledge the imbalance and take steps to correct your course.

Lastly, and arguably the most crucial aspect, is recognizing the appropriate time to bring your business venture to a close. Dream big and shoot for the moon, but don't be held hostage to your dreams or ambitions at the detriment of your interpersonal relationships and your health. Don't get me wrong. Make the necessary sacrifices and work hard toward actually achieving your goals, but keep a balance and keep yourself grounded in reality. Ask yourself along your journey, *Am I achieving my purpose? Am I enjoying this journey? Am I living according to my principles? Am I meeting my objectives?* Only you possess the knowledge of an appropriate time to conclude your entrepreneurial endeavor. However, a valuable guideline to contemplate terminating it is if you feel constantly stressed or anxious, are in a perpetual state of misery, or worse, your health is actually being affected.

In addition to these significant overarching factors, I would like to present eight additional supplementary points that should be taken into account when starting a business with your soulmate.

#1: There needs to be a strong purpose for being in business together.

If your sole purpose for being in business is simply to make money, then you will never have the willingness or resiliency to continue when faced with the difficult and uncomfortable moments that will inevitably arise. Trust me, running a business is no walk in the park. You *will* face countless challenges along the way. In order to push through those hard moments when owning a business, you must have a strong purpose for existing. The "why" of your company should not only be clearly defined for the benefit of your team members, but it should also hold a significant meaning for both you and your spouse.

For example, do not open a business that rescues stray dogs if animals in general are not really your thing. You must choose a path that resonates with your vision and values.

Both Will and I shared an equal passion for our company's mission, which was to offer dental care to children who lacked access due to insurance or medical reasons. This shared purpose was crucial as it prevented any potential conflicts between us and ensured that neither of us would give up easily when faced with challenges. When your business is driven by a meaningful and shared purpose, it provides the strength and determination needed to weather any storm that may arise.

#2: Harness the power of your mind.

A strong mindset is the foundation of any endeavor, whether your goal is to be an involved parent with your kids or to create a profitable business. Developing a strong mindset, however, does not happen overnight, nor are you necessarily born with one. Mindset is developed through experiences, especially by overcoming the negative ones. The ability to endure and overcome difficulties, pain, and challenges will ultimately sharpen and strengthen your mind. If you quit at the first sign of trouble or during an uncomfortable situation, then you will inevitably weaken your mind and train it to surrender when confronted with a challenge.

As an example, there was a time when our business faced financial difficulty and Will requested a report of new patient counts and an update on the call center, which was in a state of flux from high employee turnover. Being busy with other tasks in the business, I completely forgot to turn the requested report and action plan to him. Will was facing immense pressure to turnaround the company's operations, and in one of our meetings he reprimanded me for not turning in the requested information. The way he spoke to me seemed somewhat condescending, as if we were not equal business partners. I was so taken aback by his accusatory and callous tone that I simply left the office rather than confront him about the incident. I was in an incendiary mood and I didn't want to say something I would later regret. This incident was so impactful for me that I actually considered looking for a different job.

However, rather than make an emotional decision, I took a moment to regain my composure and think about the possible reasons behind Will's reaction toward me. Was he really being insensitive to intentionally hurt my feelings? Or, was he simply stressed from the pressures from work, especially since he had just started a new and difficult role within the company?

Rather than quit, as I initially wanted to do, I decided to speak with him about the incident in hopes of better understanding his point of view. During our conversation, he expressed remorse for the manner in which he had addressed me and acknowledged that he was under immense pressure to revitalize the company. He confided in me that there were moments when he felt as though he was not making any headway with the business. I clarified that I, too, was overwhelmed with my managerial responsibilities and had inadvertently neglected to generate the required reports. I further emphasized that this oversight was not intentional or a result of negligence on my part.

From that particular incident, we gained valuable insights into the expectations we had for each other's performance, especially during times of high stress. We discovered the importance of effective communication, setting clear expectations, and being considerate of each other's emotions. These lessons have helped us improve our working relationship and create a more supportive and understanding environment.

As a result, we deepened our understanding of each other's personality type, strengthened our bond as a married couple, and improved our relationship as business partners. In the process, we sharpened our mindsets and learned to see things from a "let's try and resolve this issue" perspective, rather than "he hurt my feelings; I'm quitting!"

#3: Perseverance is pivotal.

Similar to having a strong mindset, perseverance—the art of not taking "no" for an answer—is extremely crucial for your success. How many successful individuals do you know that have not faced challenges, adversity, or setbacks throughout their journey? The answer is... *none.*

Every accomplished individual who has achieved remarkable success in their business or has built a nurturing family has encountered numerous obstacles along their journey. What set them apart and led to their success was their unwavering perseverance, their ability to face adversity head-on, and their refusal to surrender, regardless of the challenges they faced.

An example of this is when we enlisted the services of a business consultant in 2019. He delivered the harsh reality that our company was teetering on the brink of financial ruin due to our expenses. Initially, this news felt like a devastating blow, but rather than wallow in self-pity, or quit altogether, we chose to take decisive action to rescue our business. This involved making tough choices that were necessary to steer our company away from failure and toward sustainable growth. As a result, we successfully turned the tide and continued to thrive in a profitable manner.

At home, balancing our children's demanding extracurricular schedules has been a recurring challenge for us. With their interests spanning across various activities such as gymnastics, track and field, dance, tennis, parkour, and mixed martial arts, it often felt overwhelming to juggle our work responsibilities and shuttle them to different locations. However, instead of giving in to fatigue and discouragement, we embraced the mindset that if these activities held importance for our children, they held importance for us as well. We refused to let our exhaustion or work-related stress hinder us from supporting our children in pursuing their passions. This unwavering commitment not only strengthened our familial bond but also instilled in our children a deep sense of gratitude for the sacrifices we made on their behalf.

#4: How much are you willing to sacrifice?

Unfortunately, nothing in life comes for free. In order for you to achieve success in any facet of your life, you must be willing to sacrifice. How much you are willing to sacrifice depends on your preferences and life's priorities.

For example, Will's original vision for our company was to have offices spread throughout the nation. He, however, realized that in order to fulfill that plan, he would have to sacrifice his health and time away from our family. This was a sacrifice he was not willing to make.

We did, however, sacrifice a great deal to achieve our level of success. When we decided to open our business, we postponed the purchase of our home to minimize our expenses in case things didn't go our way; we opted instead to live with my parents. We sacrificed our privacy by living at my parent's house for many years while we established our business.

Will and I also sacrificed earning a salary that was commensurate with our profession for years in order to get the company up and running. Exchanging a lucrative salary for a meager one was part of the sacrifice we both needed to make in order to become successful entrepreneurs.

#5: Understand each other's strengths and weaknesses.

To divide our roles and responsibilities both at home and at work, we needed to put our egos aside and go through the laborious task of recognizing each other's strengths and, more importantly, our weaknesses. This took some time. We were in a relationship for close to ten years before opening our business, and we had lived alone in a new city for three years while Will attended his pediatric dental residency in San Francisco. This helped us understand what made each of us tick. Living together, alone, and having to fend for ourselves really opened our eyes to how we handled various challenges and tasks. It was definitely a plus that Will and I had this time to really get to know each other, but do you have to live in a new city with your life partner prior to opening a new business or be together for years as a prerequisite for understanding each other's personalities? Absolutely not. There are numerous tests such as DiSC and Myers-Briggs that can help you better understand each other's personality traits. Also, spending time with your partner and really paying attention to their habits, needs, communication style, reaction to certain situations, etc. will give you a better understanding of their personality, and will also give you a good indication as to whether you can be compatible business partners.

At our company, we also made it a point to understand our team members' personalities. This, in turn, would aid us in being able to identify what drove our team members to work to their fullest potential. We specifically used the DiSC test at our company, and it worked wonders for us, but there are other personality tests you could use as well. The specific personality test is not important. What is vital is for you to understand your partner's personality type—and your team members' as well.

#6: Be a "productive paranoid."

During those times when everything was going well and things were finally working in our favor—the offices were busy, team morale was high, we were receiving stellar reviews, and we were generating a profit—we were tempted to simply maintain the status quo and cruise from that point forth, but we never did. As a business owner, it is always good to be a "productive paranoid" and act as if there is someone trying to outmaneuver or outwork you to take your place at the top. More than likely, your competitors are vying to make you irrelevant, especially if you experience exponential growth like we did.

During our time managing the business, Will and I were constantly aware of the fierce competition in our industry. We understood that there were other groups and offices that could potentially offer superior service, innovative ideas, creative marketing strategies, and groundbreaking solutions to their patients. Rather than capitulating to fear or complacency, we chose to embrace this awareness as a driving force for improvement and growth. This sense of healthy paranoia motivated us to continuously reinvent ourselves, constantly seeking ways to enhance our offerings, exceed customer expectations, and stay ahead of the curve. By embracing this mindset, we were able to maintain a competitive edge and ensure the long-term success of our business.

#7: Do you own a business, or do you own a *job*?

As the leader of your company, are you the controlling type that fails to delegate? Do you have systems and processes in place so that your business can operate without you being present? Do you have the right team members at your company, in the right positions, doing the right job? Have you created a work environment where your ideas are challenged, disputed, and even refuted? Or do you have "yes" people on your team that simply agree with all of your decisions? The answers to these questions determine the type of business—or job—you own.

If you are a controlling type, that has not taken the time to create proper operational processes, and has hired team members that do not challenge the status quo because of fear or negative backlash, then you simply *own a job,* and will barely have time to pursue other interests. A good business is meant to operate without the leader being present. In fact, Will and I always told our leadership team, including our office managers, that a proper litmus test of their leadership ability is how well their department or office functioned without them being present. If chaos ensued or the office came to a halt because they were absent, then this was a telltale sign of poor leadership.

Take the time also to hire quality team members, ones that truly embody your company's core principles. Do not rush this step. We have a guiding principle at work that states, "Slow to hire, fast to fire." If a team member does not demonstrate capability within his or her ninety-day probationary period, let them go and start the hiring process over again. Once you determine that the team member is a proper fit in your organization, take the time to train him properly.

Create proper systems and processes, and eliminate bottlenecks for your team. The goal with operations is to create efficiency throughout your organization. Gain the input from your team and eliminate cumbersome or redundant processes or tasks. Catalog all your core processes in standard operating manuals and train your team constantly on these best practices.

As the leader, it is your duty to create an environment that invites discord, debate, and differing opinions so that every idea is deliberated—and implemented—on the basis of its merit. Work environments where the leader has an inflated ego and is controlling, intense, and denigrating are usually prone to having "yes" people that will not disrupt the status quo for fear of retribution.

Ask yourself, *As the leader of my company, am I the only person in the room talking, engaging in long soliloquy without interruption or interjection from my team?* If you are engaging in this type of behavior, you need to release control and learn to ask for candid feedback and honest opinions from your team.

By implementing effective systems and processes within your business, you can create a self-sustaining organization that doesn't require your constant presence and decision-making. This will grant you the freedom to pursue other interests and maintain a healthy work-life balance. It is crucial to set up your company correctly from the start to avoid being consumed by the demands of running a business. By establishing efficient systems, delegating tasks, and empowering your team, you can ensure that your business operates smoothly even in your absence. This will provide you with the time and flexibility to spend with your family and nurture your marriage, allowing you to prioritize your personal life alongside your professional endeavors. Remember, achieving a work-life balance is not only possible but essential for your overall well-being and happiness.

#8: Time management.

Starting a business with your spouse while raising a family requires careful planning and balancing of responsibilities. It may initially seem overwhelming to juggle the demands of both areas of life, but it is possible with proper time management.

The first step is making a list with a hierarchy of your priorities, as I already explained. Knowing what's important to you and your life partner is crucial in determining *what* to dedicate your time to and how much time to allocate.

As a personal example, Will and I knew that our health and well-being are very important to us. Therefore, we wake up every morning at 5:00 a.m. to workout before our day starts. So we don't waste time in the morning and to keep ourselves accountable, we lay out all our gear the night before.

While running our business, I was able to manage my call center, meet with marketing executives, have brainstorming sessions with my team, *and* still manage to fulfill my mommy duties, nurture my friendships, dedicate time to achieving my fitness goals, and spend time with my husband all thanks to my diligent time management. I would schedule meetings around my kid's schedule, for example, and I would only hold a meeting if it truly held importance to me or the company. Otherwise, hosting a meeting without any clear objectives or just as a formality is what I refer to as "death by meeting."

Parting Thoughts

Richelle Peña

I AM GRATEFUL FOR the incredible life we lead as a married couple and business partners. God put two individuals of distinct cultures on the same life path. After meeting at a Halloween party hosted by the Health Professions Division at Nova Southeastern University twenty years ago, Will and I have remained inseparable.

We have observed each other's evolution from being college sweethearts to becoming young healthcare professionals, then transitioning into parenthood, and ultimately becoming entrepreneurs when we made the collective decision to unite and establish our own company.

Please understand that our journey to becoming a successful "power couple" was not an overnight transformation. It required a significant amount of time for us to truly understand each other. Along the way, we encountered numerous encumbrances, made many mistakes, and had disagreements before we discovered our individual strengths. However, once we identified these strengths, we realized how to utilize them to generate substantial value in our marriage, family and also in our business. Knowing that we have achieved this as a team is the ultimate accomplishment for us.

I also want to acknowledge a common concern that many aspiring entrepreneurs may have—where do I start? I understand that many of you may have a business idea that you're passionate about, but are hesitant to pursue it due to the responsibilities of raising children. It's also possible that you already own a business and desire to spend more time with your family, but are unsure of how to achieve that balance. Our story is intended to inspire and demonstrate that it is indeed possible to have a thriving business and a fulfilling family life, all while working alongside your soulmate.

If you are unsure of how to begin, I would recommend starting by expressing your determination to pursue your life's aspirations. Whether your objective is to establish a non-profit organization, pursue a long-held business idea, or simply find balance between your professional and personal life, affirm that it is feasible to pursue different paths in life and achieve success in all of them. This is why having the right mindset is crucial. As Alex Toussaint, my favorite Peloton instructor, often reminds me during his classes, "The minute you say you can't do something is the moment where you quit on yourself." By declaring your intentions and firmly believing in your ability to achieve them, you have taken the initial stride toward attaining your goals.

Now, I'm sure many of you are daunted by our suggestions or truthfully may not have a clue where to start. That's okay. If that's the case, I would suggest then hiring a coach that uses a holistic approach to life and will work to help you align your goals and dreams with your priorities in life.

Not wanting to engage in shameless self-promotion, I will simply suggest that you can always give Will and me a call, or send us an email at info@healthbiz-mastery.com. You can also directly message me on my Instagram page (@richellepena_) or find us on LinkedIn or our website www.healthbiz-mastery.com.

We'd be delighted to work with you to help you achieve the happiness and fulfillment you deserve. As we like to say in our consulting business, "Don't take advice from people who have never been where you are going." Will and I are proven entrepreneurs who have raised an amazing family and are dedicated to our personal health and wellness. More importantly, we want to help others achieve the same type of balance in their own lives.

From the bottom of our hearts, *thank you* for taking the time to read our story. Hopefully it has inspired you to take action and pursue your own dreams!

ACKNOWLEDGMENTS

As we have mentioned many times throughout our book, the success and triumphs we have enjoyed has been because of God's grace in our lives. We wouldn't be here without His guidance.

To our parents, your unwavering support, love, and commitment during our journey was fundamental to our success. We are deeply appreciative of everything you have done for us. Thank you for believing in us and sharing your words of wisdom during our entrepreneurial journey. You have no idea how much your advice helped us during those terrifying moments when we thought we would lose everything.

To my mom in heaven, thank you *mami* for shaping me into the compassionate and kind-hearted individual I am today. You showed me that caring for others is the best way to live. I know you are smiling down on me and are proud of all that I have accomplished. Wish you were here celebrating with us.

To my Nanay and Tatay, thank you for showing me to be humble and treat everyone with love and respect. I had front row seats to entrepreneurship and a true power couple who worked together to build a catering business in a new country. I love you!

We are also eternally grateful to our family and friends, who encouraged us to continue and supported us on our journey. We are so grateful to have you by our side. At times, we may not have shared everything that we were going through, but your companionship at get-togethers and family gatherings was so special to us. Thank you.

Although our book chronicles our journey as a married couple, and how we achieved business success while raising a family, there are many team members at our company that are worth mentioning for their valuable contributions to our company's success.

Nikki Quiñones: You are a rock-star and an incredible human being. We are so happy that our professional relationship has evolved into a genuine friendship. Thank you for believing in our company and in us, as a couple. We appreciate your loyalty, your hard work, and your commitment to the success of American Pediatric Dental Group. We couldn't have done it without you!

Dr. William Liou: We have nothing but deep admiration of your professionalism, caring nature, and commitment to advancing children's dentistry to a higher level. We were lucky to have you during the most difficult moments in our journey. Your support and most importantly, belief in Richelle and I, means the world to us. Like Nikki, we are grateful that our working relationship has morphed into a true friendship.

To our former administrative team (Julien, Nicole, Chris, Johann, and Lourdes): Although we had to make the heart-breaking decision to part ways for financial reasons, know that we sincerely appreciate your valuable contributions to the business. Each of you made an impact in our company because you believed wholeheartedly in our company's mission and vision. Your leadership inspired our team to keep persevering during the challenging and uncertain periods of our company's journey.

We also want to thank our amazing group of dedicated team leaders and dentists—our "OG's"— who not only believe in our company, but are also vocal advocates of our mission to provide compassionate dentistry to underserved communities. Tamika Freeman, Ariannis Lopez, Anacecilia Seguias, Trysha Taylor, Renee Arrazcaeta, Rosmery Franco, Mary Gruber, Ramon Sanchez, Dr. Tamara McCollum, Dr. Joel Frand, Dr. Roula Yaziji, Dr. Lizette Valiente, Dr. Sara Aza, Dr. Ana Maria Mejia, Dr. Linda Moleon, Dr. Reena Chaudari, you are all amazing professionals! Thank you for your hard work and loyalty to our company. We love you all!

Dr. Faisal Huda and Dr. Kistama Naidu: Two gentlemen whom I still consider as my brothers, despite everything that transpired between us. I have nothing but love and appreciation for everything you did for me personally and for our company. To Mr. Nurul Huda and Mrs. Shanaz Huda, I love you both deeply. From the bottom of my heart, thank you for treating me like a son when I most needed you.

Lastly, Kelly Ripa: You are someone I grew up watching on *Live with Regis and Kelly*, mainly for your amazing fashion sense and humor. I have always admired your ability to effortlessly balance your career, marriage, and motherhood. Your honest and relatable stories in your book *Live Wire: Long-Winded Short Stories*, resonated with me on a deep level, reminding me that I'm not alone in this constant juggling act. Just like you, I found myself in a situation where I had to navigate the delicate balance of working alongside my husband while raising our beautiful family. It wasn't an easy decision to make, but we were determined to make it work. Thank you for sharing your story about motherhood, marriage, family, and work which inspired me to write my own memoir.

Struggling with business challenges after years of patient care? Ready to start your own practice but lack the business training?

You are not alone.

HealthBiz Mastery is a *self-paced* online course that bridges the gap between patient care and business skills, drawing from our 25 years of experience building and scaling a healthcare business from scratch.

You will learn the fundamentals of business:

- ☑ Effective Marketing

- ☑ Basics of contracts and agreements

- ☑ Opening a business from scratch vs. Acquiring an existing business

- ☑ Financing

- ☑ Hiring Process

- ☑ How to achieve proper work/life balance

Our *MVP³ method*—Mindset, Vision, People, Process, Profitability—has guided countless practice owners to professional and personal success.

"Stop taking directions from people who have
never been where you're going."

Scan the QR code below to Sign Up Today!

www.healthbiz-mastery.com

Join HealthBiz Connect Community

A recent survey we conducted found 47% of healthcare professionals struggle with time management, and over 50% face burnout and self-care issues,

If you can relate, you're not alone!

Skip the costly consultants—**join HealthBiz Connect,** a community where you can share ideas, support one another, and find real solutions to practice management issues, giving you back time.

HealthBiz Connect bridges the gap between medical expertise and effective practice management, offering:

☑ Peer Support

☑ Business Tools and Resources

☑ Exclusive Insights

☑ Access to Industry Partners

☑ And much more!

Scan the QR code below and Join Today!

www.healthbiz-mastery/community

Why Join a Community?

- **Connect with Peers:** Share insights and solutions with fellow healthcare professionals.

- **Tailored Resources:** Access tools designed for mastering essential business skills.

- **Efficient Support:** Get advice from trusted peers and mentors.

FOLLOW US ON SOCIAL AT RICHELLEPENA_

LINKEDIN
https://www.linkedin.com/in/richellepena/
https://www.linkedin.com/in/drwilliampena/

APPENDIX

Recommended Books for Leaders and Entrepreneurs

1. *Good to Great: Why Some Companies Make the Leap and Others Don't.* Jim Collins. 2005.

2. *How the Mighty Fall and Why Some Companies Never Give In.* Jim Collins. 2009.

3. *Shoe Dog: A Memoir by the Creator of Nike.* Phil Knight. 2018.

4. *Extreme Ownership: How U.S. Navy Seals Lead and Win.* Jocko Willink and Leif Babin. 2015.

5. *Never Finished: Unshackle Your Mind and Win the War Within.* David Goggins. 2022.

6. *Can't Hurt Me: Master Your Mind and Defy the Odds.* David Goggins. 2018.

7. *The 21 Irrefutable Laws of Leadership.* John C. Maxwell. 2022.

8. *Wooden on Leadership: How to Create a Winning Organization.* John Wooden and Steve Jamison. 2005.

9. *The 7 Habits of Highly Successful People.* Stephen R. Covey. 2013.

10. *Tribal Leadership: Leveraging Natural Groups to Build a Thriving Organization.* Dave Logan, John King, et al. 2011.

11. *The E-Myth Revisited.* Michael Gerber. 1995.

12. *Traction: Get a Grip on Your Business.* Gino Wickman. 2012.

13. *Onward: How Starbucks Fought for Its Life Without Losing Its Soul.* Howard Shultz and Joanne Gordon. 2011.

14. *Mindset: The New Psychology of Success.* Carol Dweck. 2006.

15. *Rich Dad, Poor Dad.* Robert Kiyosaki. 2009.

16. *Cashflow Quadrant: Rich Dad's Guide to Financial Freedom.* Robert Kiyosaki. 2011.

17. *Start With Why: How Great Leaders Inspire Everyone to Take Action.* Simon Sinek. 2011.

18. *Conscious Capitalism.* John Mackey and Rajendra Sisodia, et al. 2014.

19. *The Happiness Advantage: How a Positive Brain Fuels Success in Work and Life.* Shawn Achor. 2018.

20. *Keep Sharp: Build a Better Brain at Any Age.* Sanjay Gupta. 2022.

21. *The Magic of Thinking Big.* David J. Schwartz. 2015.

22. *The Power of Habit: Why We Do What We Do in Life and Business.* Charles Duhigg. 2012.

23. *The One Truth: Elevate Your Mind, Unlock Your Power, Heal Your Soul.* Jon Gordon. 2023.

24. *The Energy Bus: 10 Rules to Fuel Your Life, Work, and Team with Positive Energy.* Jon Gordon. 2007.

25. *The One-Minute Manager.* Ken Blanchard and Spencer Johnson. 2015.

26. *The Five Dysfunctions of a Team: A Leadership Fable.* Patrick Lencioni. 2009.

27. *The 5 Love Languages: The Secret to Love that Lasts.* Gary Chapman. 2010.

28. *The Secret.* Rhonda Byrne. 2006.

29. *Positive Intelligence: Why Only 20% of Teams and Individuals Achieve Their True Potential and You Can Achieve Yours.* Shirzad Chamine. 2012.

30. *Be Seen: Find Your Voice, Build Your Brand, Live Your Dream.* Jen Gottlieb. 2023.

31. *Be Useful. Seven Tools for Life.* Arnold Schwarzenegger. 2023.

32. *Live Wire. Long-Winded Short Stories.* Kelly Ripa. 2022.